THE ANGER OF THE

THE ANGER OF THE GUNS

An Infantry Officer on the Western Front

JOHN NETTLETON

First published in 1979 by
WILLIAM KIMBER & CO. LIMITED
Godolphin House, 22a Queen Anne's Gate,
London, SW1H 9AE

ISBN 0 7183 0316 4

Reprinted 2003 as limited edition for private circulation only.

Typeset by Jubal Multiwrite Limited, London SE13 7SN
and printed in Great Britain by
Biddles Limited, King's Lynn

Contents

List of Illustrations

Illustrations on pages 149–52 are from a film in the Imperial War Museum. Most other illustrations were drawn from the author's photograph album, kindly supplemented by Mr William Brown.

Preface

The late John Nettleton wrote these recollections in the 1960's with no thought that they might one day be published. His family, having listened with fascination over the years to his Great War tales, asked him to write them down so that there might be a lasting and complete record for his family and friends.

The author was born of British parents in 1896 in Johannesburg, then part of the Boer republic of the Transvaal. He was sent home to England to school at St Andrew's, Eastbourne and then Rugby. He volunteered for the Army in January 1915 straight from school.

After the war he qualified as a Chartered Accountant before choosing a career with a major oil company in the Far East. His tours of duty led him to Hong Kong, where he married and his eldest son was born, Indonesia and the Philippines, where two more sons were born, French Indochina and Singapore. Escaping from Singapore within hours of the surrender to the Japanese he made his precarious way via Sumatra to Australia. Here he was eventually rejoined by his wife who had left Singapore some weeks earlier. At the Japanese surrender he returned to Singapore and then Hong Kong.

He retired to Whitstable on the Kent coast in 1949 and died in 1972, leaving a widow, three sons and eight grandchildren.

As a child, John Nettleton saw British cavalry lines ruining his parents' cherished lawn during the Boer war. He endured the worst of the First World War. He was ejected from his home and chased across the East Indies in the Second World War. It is ironic that such a pacific man should not have escaped the three major wars of this century.

What passing-bells for these who die as cattle?
  Only the monstrous anger of the guns.
Only the stuttering rifles' rapid rattle
  Can patter out their hasty orisons.
No mockeries for them from prayers or bells,
  Nor any voice of mourning save the choirs,
The shrill, demented choirs of wailing shells,
  And bugles calling for them from sad shires.

What candles may be held to speed them all?
  Not in the hands of boys, but in their eyes
  Shall shine the holy glimmers of good-byes.
The pallor of girls' brows shall be their pall;
Their flowers the tenderness of silent minds,
And each slow dusk a drawing-down of blinds.

WILFRED OWEN
Anthem for Doomed Youth

The author photographed in July 1914.

I

The New School

There has recently been a renewal of interest in the First World War and a number of books have been written about it. These, however, deal with politics and strategy and give very little information about the day to day life of the individuals who were the actual cannon-fodder. This must be so, because the only records and documents to which the historian can refer are those dealing with the more important individuals and events. The actions and feelings of the ordinary man in the line were not documented and even the accounts in the daily newspapers were not in the least realistic until Philip Gibbs began, quite late in the war, to break down the censorship and report what life in the line was really like.

I am therefore going to put down in writing what I can remember of my own experiences. I cannot, at this late date, pretend to write a coherent history even of my own personal war. I have no data to go on other than a rather muddled diary that I kept of three weeks in the line with the Naval Division in September 1916 and the official history of the 8th Division which was published in 1926. This latter gives the dates at which we were at certain places and to that extent helps one to place incidents in their correct chronological order, but the detail of some of the actions of which I have personal knowledge is so much at variance with my memory of them that my copy of the book is scored with many caustic marginal comments. However, certain incidents have impressed themselves on my memory and, trivial though many of them may be, I hope that by setting them down I may be able to give some idea of what the war was like for, at least, some of us.

To begin with it must be remembered that we were young – incredibly young. Not only in years but also, in my case and in many such cases like mine, in experience of the world. Oddly enough, this was not such a handicap as it might appear. It helped one to accept the oddities of army life without worrying too much about the whys and wherefores.

A child accepts, without question, the way of life he is born into. Whether he lives in a palace or a hovel, a nipa hut or an igloo, he accepts the way of life that he sees around him as the normal way people live. In fact, he has to be comparatively old before he even discovers that there may be any other way of life.

I spent a normal childhood in a happy family, with nurses and governesses to oversee my every move. Then prep-school where the supervision was as close and continuous. At St Andrew's (my preparatory school at Eastbourne) we only had one period a week – an hour or so on Sunday evenings – when we were allowed to do whatever we liked. Even then, we had to do something. One could stick stamps or cigarette cards in an album, read or be read to, play games or do anything within reason but one was not allowed to 'just sit'.

At Rugby there was a slight relaxation of this supervision, but it was very slight. Occasionally, on a half holiday, one could get leave off games in certain circumstances and go for a bicycle ride. One was free for a couple of hours, but even so ninety per cent of one's time was organised for one. And apart from the official school rules, there were the ridiculous 'side rules', made by the boys themselves, that laid down whether you could or could not put your hands in your trousers pockets and how one's books should be carried between the House and School, and so on. Also the 'Stodge Rules', which laid down what one could eat over and above the food supplied by one's Housemaster, and what one could not eat.

I was beaten for breaking Stodge Rules in my first term. My study companion (Handfield-Jones) had been sent a fruit cake by his mother and we were caught eating it. We knew about Stodge Rules of course, but it never occurred to either of us that it could be a crime to eat a cake sent one by one's own mother. It wasn't as though we had gone out and deliberately bought one in order to indulge in an orgy of gluttony.

The theory behind the Stodge Rules, which only applied in the winter terms, was that everyone should be in training so that he would be fit to represent his House at football at any time, if called upon to do so. The fact that two very small, inky fags had no more chance of being called upon to uphold the honour of the House than they had of flying to the moon, was neither here nor there. We had broken the rules and we were duly beaten for it. Not very hard, I must admit. Justice was quite obviously tempered with mercy, but it served notice that even the smallest and most insignificant members of the community must abide by the rules made by the community. We accepted the warning in the spirit in which it was given and the next time dainties were received from home, certain elementary precautions were taken against surprise. Thus we learnt the first rule of army (or any other) life, long before we ever thought of joining the army – 'Thou shalt not be found out'.

But the point I started to make before I got sidetracked, was that, to me, joining the army was something like going to a new school. One had to learn a new set of rules and, ridiculous though they might be, they were really no more ridiculous than the rules one had learned to live with at one's last school.

To a man who had been out in the world on his own for some time since leaving school, this was not so. The absurd side of army regulations struck him forcibly as being just plain absurd and he was naturally inclined to kick against them. That made it just that much more difficult for him to settle down and accept things as they were than for us younger men.

The other thing that makes it so difficult to write an intelligible account is the fact that one knew so very little of what was going on. Even in civil life, the average man's viewpoint and radius of action is pretty limited. But one can usually formulate, at least to oneself, some sort of reason for going from Point A to Point B and for doing whatever one does when one gets there. In the army one couldn't do that. One didn't even go from A to B – one was marched there and often for no apparent reason. Then one waited five minutes or five hours and, either way, there was no explanation. There were rumours, of course. The smaller the amount of reliable information there is available, the wilder and more numerous the rumours.

But the only time one had any real inkling of what the future had in store was when one went back a long, long way – right beyond the normal rest areas to the country behind, roughly, the Hazebrouck, St Pol, Amiens line. Then one knew that one was being 'fattened up' for the next show and could anticipate, with certainty, a lot of noisy unpleasantness in the near future.

Similarly, in the line, one knew the little bit of trench for which one was responsible; perhaps a hundred or two yards, probably less. Forward, one's view was limited to what one could see with one's eyes about a foot above the level of the parapet and less if snipers were active. One never saw a Boche and one was hardly concerned even with what went on on one's own side of No Man's Land unless it affected one's own little sector.

If, for some reason or other, the Boche started a hate on the front line on your flank, the ordinary reaction was 'The poor old So and Sos are catching it. Wonder if it will spread this way'. If the hate was on some objective behind the front line, it was merely ignored as something that didn't concern you.

'Worm's-eye view' was a joke, but it was almost literally true. Therefore the ordinary private soldier or junior subaltern's observations cannot be expected to add much to the knowledge of the higher conduct of the war.

I joined the Artists (28th Battalion London Regiment) in January 1915, when I was just over eighteen. We made our own arrangements about food and lodging and had to report to the HQ at Dukes Road, Euston Road, each morning at nine o'clock. Thence we went out to Russell Square or one of the other squares in the neighbourhood, in small squads, to learn the elementary drill. We were paid 1/- [5p] a day plus 2d a day kit allowance and another small amount, I forget how much, which was intended to cover rations and lodging.* It wasn't nearly enough to meet these expenses of course, but everybody was so keen that nobody minded paying his own expenses. I was all right as I stayed with my aunts at their flat, 22 Cyril Mansions, Battersea Park. I believe my father paid them something for my keep and so my billeting

* Charles Carrington in his book *Soldier from the Wars Returning* says that the subsistence allowance was 2/9d a day.

and ration allowances went into my own pocket and just about paid for my lunches and my fares between Battersea Park and Euston Road.

Our first introduction to army mores was when a man was slaughtered for blowing his nose while standing at attention. It happened that the CO himself was taking the parade and he made an example of this unfortunate man by ordering him to report at Dukes Road at 6 a.m. every morning for a month. We thought this very harsh. But the 'let it drip' order was just another peculiar rule of this new school and was accepted as such. A dripping nose might be ungentlemanly but it was obviously better than having to be on parade every morning at six, so we dripped.

There were no uniforms for the first few weeks and when they did arrive, they were horrible. Not only scratchy and uncomfortable, but far too big, at least for me. The official peace-time height limit for the regiment was 5'10" and I was only 5'7" on tiptoe. (The MO spotted that I was on tiptoe when I was being examined on enlistment, but let it pass.) The result was that my trousers bagged over the top of my puttees almost down to the ankles and I was known for sometime as 'Funny little François with the baggy bags'.

I didn't care what I looked like at Dukes Road with all the others, most of whose uniforms only fitted where they touched, but I had to go up and down by tube amongst civilised people and I was so ashamed that I kept putting off wearing my uniform on one excuse or another until I was finally told that if I turned up in civvies once more I would be put on a charge.

After uniforms had been issued and we had learnt to distinguish our right hands from our left, we were marched up to Hampstead Heath every day for more advanced work. It was still very early days and troops of any sort, even the Artists, were potential heroes. We nearly always halted for a breather halfway up Haverstock Hill and people used to come out of their houses and present us with chocolate and cigarettes. And once, waiting on a tube station on our way home, a dear old lady came up to my great friend Brown (we called him 'Bruin') and pressed a shilling into his hand 'because he had a nice face'. He was so flabbergasted

The author (*with pipe*) with a fellow recruit in the Artists' Rifles January 1915 at The Spaniards, Hampstead Heath and (*right*) W. Brown (Bruin) who had a shilling pressed into his hand 'because he had a nice face'.

that he could only stand with his mouth open, looking at the shilling until long after she had gone.

We were also highly respectable. I remember the battalion being made to march to attention because we were singing a lewd song ('Hullo, Hullo, Who's Your Lady Friend') in a respectable neighbourhood.

The training we did on Hampstead Heath was almost all picket and outpost work, based on the Boer War tactics, varied by some trench digging. One of our officers was Sir Somebody Something Bart, who was an agriculturally minded gentleman, clearly more at ease tramping round his farm with his gun on his shoulder and his dog at his heels than as a military instructor. He had a slight stammer and began every sentence with 'O'. At that time the open-topped buses all had a notice at the top of the steps which said 'To stop the O'bus, ring bell once'. From this, the old boy was nicknamed 'The O'Bus'.

One of his more famous remarks, about outpost duty, was: 'O, who is it you've got to know where they are now?' Nobody could think of the answer, because nobody knew what on earth he meant, till B.A.R. Shore earned momentary fame by working it out and giving the required answer which was that, when you were on outpost duty, you had to know where your picket was and where the outposts on your left and right were.

Apart from Hampstead Heath we were sometimes taken farther afield. One such do was at High Beech in Epping Forest. This was a pub that, in peace-time, was a great favourite for East End bean feasts. I forget why we went there, but I remember that we were all sleeping on the floor of a big dance-hall attached to the pub, which contained a huge mechanical organ. Sometime after lights out, someone put a shilling in this infernal machine and it blared out fairground music that fairly woke the echoes. Sergeants cursed and shouted, officers came over from their billets, but nobody knew how to stop it and for an hour bedlam reigned.

Another incident concerned a draft for France which was paraded for inspection by the GOC London Command (General Lloyd). It was supposed to be *en état de partir*, that is, with everything complete right down to the last pair of spare bootlaces, ready, if need be, to march straight off parade into battle.

After the formal inspection, a considerable number of men, picked out at random, were ordered to take off their equipment and spread it all out for kit inspection. The result was embarrassing. Many of the beautifully squared packs had been made trim with pieces of wood down the sides and were filled with hay as being less burdensome than greatcoat and complete kit. The General went purple in the face (he was alleged to wear stays) and cursed us as the most unmitigated set of sweeps he had ever had under his command and the CO looked as though he wanted to crawl under the nearest stone. I expect he got into a good deal of trouble over the incident, but to us it was merely amusing. If one's platoon sergeant had cause to be dissatisfied with one's conduct, he could make life unpleasant, but generals were so far above us that their ravings were no more important to us than the growl of distant thunder.

Other expeditions were to Rainham, on the Essex marshes on the North Bank of the Thames Estuary, for shooting. I did reasonably well at this because I had already done a good deal of full-bore shooting at Rugby. But I failed to get my marksmanship badge by one point when I was almost certain of it. We were firing individually, with fixed swords*, and when I came to my last round, I only needed a magpie. Just as I was squeezing the trigger, there was the hell of an explosion in my left ear, which made me jerk so that I only got an outer. What had happened was that the man on my left (B.R. Hilder) had not fixed his sword properly, so that the ring projected slightly over the muzzle of his rifle instead of fitting round the outside. When he fired his first shot, the bullet caught the edge of the sword ring and blew off the sword and burst the front edge of the muzzle of the rifle in what might have been a nasty accident.

In April 1915 we moved, for the first time as a complete unit, to Roehampton House, Roehampton Lane. We marched in style from Dukes Road, headed by our own drums and fifes all across London. I remember being impressed at having to break step on Hammersmith Bridge. It seemed impossible that a great big bridge, that could carry dozens of buses and heavy lorries, could be set

* Rifle regiment terminology for bayonet.

Training with the Artists' Rifles.

swinging dangerously by a few hundred men. On arrival and while we were waiting to be dismissed, I felt faint and had to put my head between my knees. That was the only time I ever had to fall out on a march.

Roehampton House was quite new, when we moved in. So new in fact that the floors had not been laid in a few of the upper rooms. And not long after it was taken over as a hospital for men needing artificial limbs and has been used for that purpose ever since. So the private owner who built it can never have got much use out of what would have been a most lovely home.

After two or three weeks, we moved into tents in Richmond Park, where the public golf course now is. It was a big camp; there were five territorial battalions there – the Artists, London Scottish, Queen's Westminsters, City of London Fusiliers and one other, whose name I forget. Accommodation was in bell tents with about twelve men to a tent, who slept spread out like the spokes of a wheel with their feet towards the tent pole at the centre. That meant that one's 'home' was a space about six feet long by three feet wide in which one lived and ate and slept and had one's being. There were no tent boards, but we had blankets and, though the conditions were new to most of us, they were not too bad.

Washing accommodation consisted of long wooden troughs with cold taps at intervals along them. No baths and no hot water, but the people living round the park were very good about letting us use their bathrooms. I was better off than most people, because I could go to the Aunts' flat at Battersea and have a bath any time I could get an hour or two off.

We plunged at once into violent training for which we were nothing like ready. The day started at 5.30 a.m. with PT and a nice run round the park. But this caused so many casualties at first that it had to be reduced to PT or a run, not both, and an issue of biscuits and tea was made before we started. Then we worked at field exercises and route marches till about 4.30 and were usually free after that. The favourite amusement of our particular crowd was a fish supper at Sam Isaacs in Putney High Street and a cinema or a stroll along the river. Taxis reaped a harvest by running a shuttle service down Priory Lane from the Upper

Practising at Ham shooting range summer 1915.

Richmond Road to the park gates at 6d a head with perhaps a dozen men in and on the machine.

What I found most trying was the lack of sleep. Lights out was at 10.00 p.m.. and reveille at 5.30 a.m. Each battalion took it in turn to wake the camp up after reveille with its own band. Ours always played 'It's nice to get up in the morning in the good old summer time' and I learned to hate that tune. However tired you were, it was no good trying to go to bed early, because people would be trampling about on your face trying to get their bedding laid out, until the very last moment.

Shortly after moving into camp, I joined the Scout Section with, amongst others, B.A.R. Shore, B.R. Hilder, and N.R. Clarke. B.A.R. was a St Paul's boy of my own age, who had joined the Artists on the same day as myself. He was a musician in a very real sense. Hilder was also a musician, the organist of a church at Hunstanton. He was older than us and had quite white hair though he was well under thirty. He also had a bad stutter which prevented him from taking a commission. Clarke was still older; he must have been over thirty and his great age made him a sort of benevolent uncle to the rest of us.

In the Scout Section, I got the only military training that was of any practical use. We used to go out all day, ranging over the country round Epsom, Mitcham and Sutton, and I think we knew every pub in that area. We learned to read maps, use a compass, judge distance, write intelligible reports and generally acquire an eye for country. We even went out and lived on the country for two or three days, somewhere round Mitcham. It is all covered with houses now, but we camped out under a hedge, pulled mangel-wurzels out of a field and incorporated them in a very nasty stew that we made with bully-beef in our mess tins. We were also supposed to make a sort of unleavened bread, by mixing flour which we carried, with water and then cooking it over the fire. The flour and water was mixed on someone's tunic which was spread out on the ground. The theory was that if the flour and water was mixed in the right proportions, what was left on the tunic after the small loaves had been lifted off would just be a little dry flour that could easily be shaken off. Owing to our inexperience, it didn't work out like that. What was left after the

The Scouts Section 2nd Battalion Artists' Rifles in Richmond Park July 1915. The author is standing third from the right, in the back row: 'I was only 5'7" on tiptoe.' In the front row, fourth from the left is B.R. Hilder, sixth from the left N.A. Clarke and the second from the right is B.A.R. Shore.

Striking camp at Richmond Park. W. Brown is handling the tent pole.

loaves had been lifted off was a glutinous mess that couldn't be shaken, or even scraped off. I was very glad I had not volunteered to lend my tunic for the experiment.

II

France

All this time of course we were getting fitter. Nevertheless, the first time we were made to carry packs, even though we only put our greatcoats in them and not our full kit, we all lay down and groaned in agony after the first half mile. Muscles you didn't know you had screamed in protest. But they got educated up to their burden in time and I must say that I think the British Army's web equipment was superlatively good – much better than any other army had. It enabled a man to carry a very considerable weight as easily as it could be carried. Whether it is really desirable to require a fighting soldier to lug so much stuff about on his person is another question. In Marching Order, an infantryman carried between 70 and 80 lbs but this does not include all the extra S.A.A., bombs, sand-bags, signal lights and extra rations often carried when going into an attack.

One other item of interest is that, owing to the shortage of small arms, we were issued with Japanese rifles. They had a bolt action like ours, but it was all enclosed. When you twisted a metal rose at the back of the action, the whole thing came adrift and dozens of tiny springs and odd bits of metal shot out at you. It took about five seconds to take the thing to pieces and about five hours to re-assemble it – more if you had not taken the precaution to spread a towel or a piece of paper on the ground to catch the bits and pieces that sprang out. They were beautiful toys, but quite useless under war conditions.

By the beginning of August, we were considered fit enough for France and I and most of my friends were put on a draft to join the 1st Battalion. We marched to Barnes station and entrained for Southampton, where we went into camp just outside the town. We did no work, but odd fatigues, and were kept in camp awaiting embarkation orders. If no orders had come through by about three o'clock, it was considered that we would not be going that day and we were let out.

Every night for a week was our 'last night in England' and we went out on the spree. When orders did come through, I was quite glad, because I had spent all my money and the excitement was wearing thin.

We finally embarked about ten o'clock at night and crept out of Southampton in pitch darkness. At one time we were suddenly illumined by a glare of searchlights. It puzzled me as to how they could pick us up directly as they did, because there was no wavering about while they looked for us. One moment everything was pitch black and the next moment we were almost blinded by the glare.

B.A.R. and I found a hard, but warm spot in the lee of the funnel-casing and passed the night talking and dozing. As usual, we had no idea where we were going, but when daylight came, found we were at Le Havre. We did not disembark there, but proceeded up the Seine to Rouen. The weather was warm and sunny and it was a lovely trip. The country on the west of the river was rather uninteresting, but on the other bank there were lots of quite steep bluffs, with villages nestling at their feet and all the way people came out and cheered and waved to us.

We arrived at Rouen in the late evening and were marched up to a transit camp on top of a hill overlooking the town. The tents must have been a Crimean War issue, because they were rotten all through. In the middle of the night a thunderstorm blew up and the tents blew down. We fought our way out from under the wet flapping canvas and tried to put the tents up again, but the guy ropes wouldn't hold and we floundered about in a sea of mud in the dark without being able to accomplish anything useful.

However, when the sun came up, it stayed up and we soon dried off and spent the morning getting the mud off our rifles, clothes and ourselves.

In the afternoon, we were marched down to the station and were introduced to the pleasures of Continental rail travel. This, as conducted by the Army, was a sport of its own, the like of which I have not experienced elsewhere. The trucks were commodious and well-ventilated, each marked 'Chevaux 8. Hommes 40.' The trains never went at more than ten miles an hour and there were long unexplained stops in the middle of nowhere. These were the signal for everyone to go up to the engine to get hot water for making tea. I remember one man trying to get back to his own truck just as the train started after one of these stops. He was in his stockinged feet and had a mess tin of hot water in each hand. The train was gathering speed only very slowly and he could easily have caught it if he had dumped his precious hot water and run for it. But this he refused to do and I can still see him hobbling along as fast as he could without spilling the water, while the train slowly forged ahead of him. What happened to him, I don't know, but one of the Railway Transport Officers' ever-present problems was dealing with odd bodies like this, who had lost their units and their rifles and their kit and had no idea where they were or where they were meant to be going.

It was really very pleasant to sit in the open doorway of the truck with your legs dangling over the side, watching the fair land of France go past so slowly that you could see every detail and shout greetings to the people by the wayside. I have no idea how long the journey took, but, eventually, we arrived at St Omer and joined our 1st Battalion.

The 1st Battalion of the Artists was one of the first territorial units to go to France. It was composed of men keen enough on things military to have enlisted and been trained in peace-time. Because of the heavy casualties amongst junior officers in the early part of the war, a number of these men were given emergency commissions in the field. They were a great success, so the battalion was withdrawn from the line and sent back to GHQ to form a sort of unofficial reserve of potential officers. We didn't know this when we joined, but it was very lucky for us because it meant that we had a long stay in the back areas instead of being pitched headlong into the unpleasant part of the war.

Anyway, the Artists were now GHQ Troops which meant, in effect, that they had to provide guards and do all the odd jobs at GHQ. The guards were the main job. We had a ceremonial guard mounting parade in the Grande Place every morning which required about 250 men. We had guards on all the seven roads that radiated out of St Omer like the spokes of a wheel, on several of the HQ offices and on Sir John French's personal billet. In addition we had to provide guards of honour when politicians or other big-wigs came to visit.

As soon as we found out how things were, some of us who did not particularly care for the ceremonial side of Army life, joined the Signal Section. With me in this, were B.A.R., Hilder, Clarke, Bruin and Cates. As specialists, we were supposed to devote our time to our own speciality and were not called on for general duties unless there was a great shortage of men. We also had to provide a permanent bicycle orderly for our own Orderly Room and two or three for the Office of the Brigadier Commanding HQ Troops. This was the office that looked after pay, rations, billeting and general administration of all the GHQ personnel – clerks etc. – also such bodies as the GHQ Reserve Ammunition Train and the GHQ Reserve Bus Park. This last, incidentally, was composed of a hundred or so London buses, some still in their original colours and bearing their original advertisements, though they all got painted a uniform subfusc colour before long.

At first there was some friction in the Signal Section between the old hands and the newcomers. They thought we were a lot of namby-pamby twerps and we thought they were a lot of drunken louts. However, by dint of living and working together, the rough edges were rubbed off both factions and we settled down to become a first class unit of blackguards, loyal to each other and agin everyone else – especially the authorities.

We were quartered in a French peacetime barracks, a proper weather-proof building, but deficient in washing and sanitary facilities. We had two large rooms furnished somewhat sparsely with rifle racks and a table in each. But by this time we were good enough soldiers to realise that a soldier's first duty is to look after his own comfort and soon some timber was 'acquired' and rough cots constructed. They were just frames and the 'bed' consisted of one's waterproof sheet spread across the top and hooked on to the side members by slipping the eyelet holes over nails protruding from the side pieces. The most remarkable thing about them was the way the waterproof sheets stood up to the strain. How many waterproof sheets that you could buy today would support the weight of a man and his blankets simply by their own tensile strength, with nothing whatever underneath them?

The next advance towards home comforts was to tell the cooks we didn't like the messes they concocted and preferred to draw our rations uncooked. Then we bought two or three primus stoves. Petrol for these could be purchased from the Army Service Corps drivers whose lorries were parked in the barrack courtyard. They used it themselves to wash their overalls in and made no difficulty about giving us enough to fill all our primus stoves in exchange for a packet of cigarettes.

It was the duty of the NCO who had to get up at reveille to report the Signal Section present, to start a panful of porridge on one of the primuses. By the time the rest of us got up an hour or so later, the porridge was ready. This was followed by bacon and eggs, which each man cooked for himself.

The bacon was part of our ration and peasant women bringing their goods to market would supply us with eggs by means of a basket let down on a string from a window on the outer side of the barracks.

Our midday meal was usually taken outside in picnic form and in the evening one ran up some simple dish like Welsh Rabbit for oneself or dined out.

Of course, we didn't get away with this all the time. On one occasion, our officer (Lieutenant Adams) was surprised to find most of us still in bed when he arrived about eight o'clock and laid about violently at the recumbent bodies with his swagger-stick. We had to fall in line for a bit after that, but things soon settled down again.

While we did not conform very well to the ordinary ideas of discipline, we were always very careful to see that nobody had any cause for complaint against the section itself. We made sure that the work we had to do was done, though we made our own arrangements for doing it. If a man wasn't on the job when he ought to have been, someone else did it and organised a reciprocal swap with the defaulter later. Thus, if you wanted to go out when it was your turn on Orderly Room duty, you could usually find someone who wanted to stay in to write letters or something. If a job turned up and it was a small one such as taking a message to some nearby office, he would do it. If the job was a long one such as taking a message round all the perimeter posts – which took over an hour – he would come and find you in your usual haunt and hand the job over to you to complete.

Similarly, the NCO on duty always reported the section present and complete at Lights Out. If you were not in barracks by then, it was up to you to get in, without giving the show away, and this was not too difficult as there were always signallers out on legitimate duties, taking messages or returning after a shift at the Brigade office.

We also made things easier for ourselves by fitting up a two-way switchboard from the Orderly Room to our Section Room. This was a minor work of genius constructed by Sergeant Cook. The telephone wires were soldered on to bullets which were plugged in to empty cartridge cases, fitted up on a board, as required to make the connections. This meant that the orderly on duty could lie on his own bed and read or write until he was required instead of having to sit, fully dressed, in the Orderly Room itself. The Regimental Sergeant Major didn't like it as he had to move a switch at his end one way to ring us up and another way to talk and he always forgot in which position the switch had been left. It was easier for him, when the orderly on duty was within shouting distance, but his objections were overcome by the plea that it was excellent technical training for us to make and use such things.

Because we were specialists, we did not often get put on ordinary guard duties. But whenever a politician or other big-wig paid a visit to GHQ, there was always a panic to get together enough men to provide a guard of honour. As soon as the warning was received the gates would be shut and the Orderly Sergeant would come round gathering up all the bodies available – room orderlies, for example, or men who had been on guard during the previous twenty-four hours and who were supposed to be having a day off. We had two main counters for this, and since we had our own men in the Brigade office from which the order would come, we knew about it at least as soon as our Orderly Room, if not before, and could get our counter-preparations under way.

The first of these was to seize flags and form up under any NCO available and march out as though we were going for training. The Guard would stop any individuals trying to get out of barracks, but would not interfere with a formed body of troops. Then we would stack our flags in the canteen outside the barracks and go our several ways down town.

The other was to dismantle two or three of our bicycles and spread the bits and pieces about all over the floor. It is surprising what a mess you can make with a few bicycles, especially if you dismantle the hubs and spread the ball-bearings all round. When the Orderly Sergeant appeared, looking for men, our NCO would be very apologetic: 'Sorry, Sergeant, but you can see what a mess we are in. I must get these bicycles serviceable before tea and I have only these men to do it with. I am afraid I can't spare anyone.' Then we would sit and smoke till the danger was past and we could safely put the pieces together and go off on our own affairs.

One of the worst of the minor horrors of war was the cleaning of dixies. The means provided was one cold tap and one pile of sand beside it. This had to serve the whole battalion and of course the sand got greasier and greasier. If you want to be thoroughly unhappy, try cleaning a dixie half full of stew out of doors in the dark and cold of a December evening with frozen hands and a pile of wet sand that is eighty per cent grease from previous use.

We tried everything we could think of to dodge this job. We bribed the ASC men, who lived in lorries in the courtyard, to do it for us. But they didn't do it properly and the cooks threw the dixies back at us as being insufficiently cleaned. We tried just dumping the things under the lorries, leaving the cooks to search for them. But the cooks retaliated by keeping a check on which sections had or had not returned their dixies. It was a problem which we never solved till we took to drawing our rations uncooked and I think it is the memory of this that has given me my distaste for washing up now, even with plenty of hot water and detergent.

The only enemy action we had to contend with was air-raids. They were on a very minor scale, of course, being quite a new sort of warfare. They were conducted by single planes that used to come over at a great height and sweep down only when they were over the town. If they could get the tower of the Cathedral, at the top of the town, lined up with the Tour St Bertin (a ruined church) at the bottom of the town and drop their bombs half way between the two, they could hit Sir John French's personal billet. There was no such thing as scientific bomb-aiming, of course. The observer just lent over the side and dropped his bomb from his hand when he thought he was about in the right place, but they made surprisingly good attempts and the front of Sir John French's billet was scarred and chipped with splinters from bombs that had dropped in the road just outside the house.

They were only 2 lb bombs that could do little material damage, but they were powerful enough to be lethal to any human beings caught in the open. I was riding round the posts one night with the air-raid warning when I came across two very small children who had been caught like this outside their home. They were lying in the gutter and one had his leg blown off. It was very unpleasant and I had to get off my bike and be sick. That was my first introduction to the real war.

Air-raid precautions were practically non-existent. I don't think there were any AA guns at that time and the standing orders were that on receipt of an air-raid warning, guards were to turn out and fire at the plane with their rifles, if they could see it. As the only communication with the posts was by means of a signaller on a bicycle and as it took more than an hour to get round to all the posts, it is not surprising that no planes were brought down by our efforts.

One moonlit night though, when you could actually see the attacking plane, I had to go to Sir John French's billet and I saw the old chap leaning out of his window to watch, with a night-cap on his head. He looked like a *Punch* illustration from about 1860.

Security arrangements were also pretty primitive as far as we could see. No one was allowed to enter the town without a pass and the main job of our posts on the roads into the town was inspecting these passes. But as they were only pieces of paper signed by people whose signatures we didn't know, any competent spy should have been able to furnish himself with a pass good enough to deceive our sentries. Alternatively, he could have nipped through somebody's back garden and dodged the posts altogether.

We did have one brush with the authorities though, when we were practising signalling with lamps after dark across the barrack yard from one room on the first floor to the corresponding room opposite. We had put our lamps right at the back of each room, but even so, somebody spotted the reflection of the flashes. The first we knew of it was when the door of the room was flung open and a voice said, 'They are our own men, sir.' It was the Regimental Sergeant Major and with him was an officer with a drawn revolver and two MP's. The most embarrassing part was that someone had taken down all the ribald messages we had been passing to each other. The chit-chat had seemed funny enough when we were sending it, but when solemnly read out in cold blood the next day, it sounded appallingly silly. Like family conversation at the dinner table does when it is recorded on tape and later played back.

By this time we were reasonably expert at morse and semaphore and most of us had our flags up, which meant that a grateful country paid us an additional 3d or 6d a day. Apart from learning morse, the training was not difficult. We had flags, lamps, buzzers and field telephones – no walky-talkies or any sort of radio; in fact nothing sufficiently complicated to give one a headache. But we did have a heliograph. Not that a heliograph is a particularly reliable means of communication in Northern Europe, but when the sun did shine, it was fun playing with it. I wonder if such things are ever used in the army nowadays?

One other job the Artists had was acting as nursemaids to a number of young soldiers. These were boys of fifteen and sixteen, who had given false ages on enlistment and who were big enough to deceive the doctors that they were eighteen or pretty near it. But, in spite of their enthusiasm, many of them were physically unable to stand the rigours of life in the line. By the winter of 1915, they were being weeded out, one by one, and were sent down to us until they could be sent home in batches. On Christmas Day, they all got drunk on French beer, watery stuff though it was, and we picked them out of the gutters and put them to bed by dozens.

Our evenings were usually free and each little group in the section had its own particular haunt, so that you always knew where to find a man if you wanted him. Our gang, consisting of Clark, Hilder, B.A.R., Bruin and myself, frequented a pastry-cook's shop in the Rue de Dunkerque owned by the Decriems. The family consisted of Papa and Maman, two sons who were away, serving in the French Army, and two daughters, Adrienne and Genevieve.

Papa was a troglodyte who lived in a cave under the shop. He only emerged to shake hands and then disappeared again. But he was a most skilful pastry cook and produced little cream cakes that tasted like angels' kisses and melted in your mouth. After Mass on Sundays, the matrons of the town used to come in and stuff themselves with these at five centimes a time.

Maman was a stout, motherly old soul who ran the shop and the family. She was very strict with her daughters, but very kind to us. I remember that once some soldier left a vulgar comic in the shop with line drawings of ladies with big breasts and buttocks. Madame confiscated it at once as being quite unfit for her daughters to read.

Adrienne was about 21, but very quiet and '*toujours triste*' because her fiancé had been killed at the front. Genevieve must have been sixteen or seventeen and was like a little kitten.

The premises consisted, first of a shop with a counter at which cakes were sold and a couple of tables with chairs. Behind the shop and opening from it was a small room with tables and chairs, where people were served with coffee and chocolate. Behind this again was another room which was used as the family sitting room. Its only ventilation was through the other two rooms in front of it, so the air was apt to be vitiated. In this atmosphere the girls lived practically all the time. I don't think they ever went out into the fresh air, except for a ceremonial promenade in the Jardin Publique for one hour on Sunday mornings; no wonder they always looked so pale and waxen.

When we first went there, we sat in the second room and drank chocolate that Madame made so rich that the spoon practically stood upright in it. But after a trial period, we were admitted to the third room, the family's own sitting room, and were considered friends rather than just customers. Anyone who has ever lived in barracks will know what it meant to us to get a bit of home life and a place in a family where we felt we belonged and we all appreciated very deeply what the Decriems did for us. On Christmas Day we had a party. We provided the food and drink and Madame cooked it and we dined in state in the parlour on the first floor. (That is the only time we saw that room, which was kept for special occasions.) It was a great success and even Papa appeared for long enough to take a drink and shake hands all round.

While the Decriems were particularly good to our little group, the Artists, as a whole, got on very well with the townspeople and established a reputation for themselves. One or two of the posts were situated in *estaminets* and it was the custom that if a man wanted a drink to warm himself upon coming in after his two-hour shift on sentry duty, he just helped himself and paid for it in the morning. The owners never thought of locking the drinks up and this arrangement worked happily for everyone, (though there was a story that it was tried later with another regiment with the result that the whole guard got drunk and smashed the place up).

Again, some months after we had moved to Hesdin, two or three of us bicycled back to St Omer and were welcomed with open arms by everyone – not only our own particular friends. Our cap-badge was a passport everywhere in the town and I don't think any of us paid for a drink or a meal during the whole day. We just weren't allowed to. And yet one hears a lot of uninformed talk about the meanness and penny-pinching ways of 'the darned frogs'. The French peasants and petty tradesmen are certainly careful about money; they have precious little of it and have to work desperately hard for that they do get. And to have an alien army quartered on you is annoying, to say the least of it. Yet reasonably decent behaviour by the soldiers brings an immediate response from the civilians, in France, as in other countries, and the response is accurately proportioned to the conduct that calls it forth. For example, a British officer's cheque could be cashed in any little village in Northern France, without question, because it was a trustworthy document, until the Australian and Canadian forces spoilt the whole friendly set-up by giving worthless cheques. After they had been stung once or twice, the small shop-keepers and *estaminet* proprietors could hardly be blamed for refusing

The Artists' Rifles at St. Omer, September 1915.

A scene at St. Omer in more peaceful times.

to cash any more cheques. It was the obvious and reasonable response to the deteriorating conduct of the troops.

One can find meanness in any nation, if one looks for it, but one has to look for it just as hard in France as in any other country.

Sir Douglas Haig took over as C-in-C just before Christmas 1915 and Sir John French went home. It didn't make much difference to us except that Clarke got reported for failing to salute Sir Douglas Haig properly. At any time, it was quite difficult to do the thing because you had to spot that it was the C-in-C's car, come to attention, slope arms and present arms before the car had passed you. In this case, it was a very cold day, Clarke's hands were half frozen and he fumbled and didn't get to the 'present' until the car was well past. The car was stopped, an ADC was sent back to get the sentry's name, and Nobby came up before the CO. It was bad luck on him, but when the Commander-in-Chief reports a private soldier, his CO can't just dismiss the case, however sympathetic he may feel privately, so Clarke got fourteen days CB and it was reported back to GHQ that 'the necessary disciplinary action had been taken'.

It must have been in the early part of December 1915 that I got my first leave, which was absurd as I had only been in France for three or four months. It was grossly unfair that a battalion sitting comfortably in weatherproof barracks, as we were, should get the same allotment of leave places as a battalion in the line. This eventually penetrated even the thick heads of the staff and the leave allotment to base units was drastically cut down, with the result that I did not get my next leave for another eighteen months, but it ought not to have taken them a year and a half to work it out.

My people were living at Cheltenham and I went down from London in the newspaper train, arriving about five in the morning, so that I had to throw gravel at bedroom windows to wake someone up to let me in. Then I usually went to bed and slept for about twenty-four hours. I forget whether I did this on my first leave, but I know I did on all my others. That did me a lot of good. So did getting out of uniform. Someone told me that one was not supposed to wear civilian clothes, but I didn't see how anyone could find out and did not worry about it. And by that time, silly girls had given up the trick of presenting white feathers to men in civilian clothes whom they thought should be in khaki.

I cannot remember any details of that first leave except the journey back to France. The leave train left Victoria at seven a.m., which meant I had to leave Cheltenham the day before and spend the night in London. Seven o'clock in the morning was a grim hour in mid-winter and everybody felt that it was. Moreover, the handling of the troops returning from leave did not help to raise morale.

At Folkestone, there was, and still is, a crescent of boarding houses on the low ground below the east end of the Leas and this was surrounded with barbed wire and turned into a concentration camp. Troops were marched direct to this camp from the station and kept there until the boat sailed, which might be in two hours or ten. The houses were empty and there was nothing to do but sit about on the floor and wish the war was over.

The authorities were afraid that if the troops were allowed loose in the town they just wouldn't turn up at the boat or would get drunk and go on the rampage. Going back to France after leave was such an unpleasant ordeal that their fears may have been well-grounded, but I think some scheme less reminiscent of slave-driving could have been devised.

On this occasion, we didn't get away till the afternoon. There was a gale blowing with high seas and the ship was so full that we were standing in packed lines on the deck and one couldn't even get to the rail to be sick.

We made no less than three attempts to get into Boulogne Harbour and we were soaked with spray right through our great-coats and all our other clothes. It was long after dark by the time we landed and we were marched up the hill to a tented camp on the high ground by the castle above the town. Because it was so late, all the camp staff except the Orderly Sergeant had gone home to their billets and there was no food or hot drink available. This was a blow, because all we had had since breakfast was the 'un-expended portion of the day's ration', most of which had been eaten at Folkestone. We did get one blanket apiece and were then herded into the tents to get what sleep we could.

That was the sort of thing that made the troops so angry with the 'base wallahs'. They knew why the leave boat was late and anyone with any imagination would know that troops would come off it tired and wet and hungry and the camp staff should have seen that there was hot food and drink available. If they didn't like doing a bit of overtime, they should have been sent up the line. There were plenty of men in the line who would have been glad to change places with them, even if it did mean working rather more than office hours.

What saved my life was that my Mum had sent me off with some ham sandwiches wrapped up in grease-proof paper. The sandwiches had been eaten long since, but I spread the nice fatty, buttery, grease-proof paper over my stomach under my shirt and it made a lovely warm layer that I am convinced saved me from a bad chill. My 'innards' were always the part of me that succumbed most easily to cold and wet, but in this fairly severe test, they never made any sort of fuss.

One interesting job the regiment did was during the battle of Loos towards the end of September 1915. We – the whole battalion – were taken to some rail-head, whose name I forget, and were set to work taking defective American fuses off 3-inch shells and fitting British fuses. It was a matter of some urgency, which one would think should have been attended to before the battle started, but that did not concern us. Our job was to take the shells out of railway trucks in a siding, carry them into a shed, change the fuses and carry the shells out to lorries waiting on the other side of the shed, which took them straight up the line. The carrying to and from the shed was the heaviest part of the work. Inside the shed, the work was organised on factory lines. We sat at trestle tables and one man did one part of the operation and rolled the shell on to the next man, who did another part of it and so on.

The work was not unduly arduous, as one got relief from the carrying when one's turn came to sit at the tables. We worked eight hours on and eight hours off. That does not sound too bad, but it was interesting to note the cumulative effects of fatigue. For instance, if one started at 8 a.m. one came off at 4 p.m., feeling perhaps that one had done a good day's work but not unduly tired. One had enough energy left to take a walk round the village and see what was going on, wash and clean up a bit and have a meal. By eight o'clock, one got down to trying to get a bit of sleep, but as the bed was a concrete floor with one blanket only, to each man, one spent more time trying to find a soft piece of concrete than actually sleeping.

On again at midnight, not much refreshed. By eight o'clock the next morning, everyone was beginning to feel a bit exhausted and no one wasted more time over breakfast and shaving than was necessary. The concrete was still infernally hard, but 4 p.m. came round all too soon. By midnight, one was really tired and going on again at 8 a.m. seemed really hard work. And so it went on for about a week and by the end of it, we were just dropping down as soon as we came off and did not even notice that we were sleeping on concrete.

All we saw of the battle of Loos was some walking wounded, who were brought down to the railhead in the empty ammunition lorries. One man, I remember, was stark naked, except for a blanket, and it did occur to me that the medical evacuation services did not appear to be working as well as they should have been. Nights at the end of September are beginning to get chilly and an open lorry is not a very comfortable conveyance for a wounded man, clothed only in a blanket.

In the early spring of 1916, GHQ moved to Montreuil, which is a walled town set on a small, but precipitous hillock. It only had one access road, so it was much easier to control people going in and out than at St Omer. The move took some days, but, just to show that they knew all about it, the Boche bombed Montreuil on the very day that Haig himself moved in.

The Artists moved also, two companies going to Montreuil and two companies and Battalion HQ to Hesdin. An advance party was send down to take over the barracks and found themselves faced with a tough job. The barracks had been used to house Belgian refugees, who had behaved just like animals. They never, apparently, bothered to go outside to the latrines, but just relieved themselves where they lived. When it got so filthy that even they noticed it, they just put down another layer of straw and proceeded to defile that also. Thus, our advance party had a cleaning up operation similar to Hercules's task in the Augean stables. Only

Artists' Rifles signallers at Hesdin, July 1916.
In the back row are G.E. Cates, awarded a posthumous V.C, and N.R. Clarke.
In the front row are W. Brown, B.A.R. Shore and the author.

A second photograph of the signallers in the previous illustration. In the back row are the author and B.A.R. Shore. In the front row are N.R. Clarke, G.E. Cates and W. Brown.
This photograph was in W. Brown's wallet in his left hand tunic pocket when he went 'over the top' in an attack and was hit by a bullet. 'It only grazed my chest with a thump – and put me in hospital for a week before I was invalided home – but without any sound. It missed by a hair's breadth as the bullet fire came *sideways* as we went forward – what a mercy.'

our people could not turn a river through the barracks; they had to clean it out themselves with pitchforks and shovels.

In addition to their share of this job, our own advance party of the Signal Section found an RE dump on the far side of the parade ground and, by the time the rest of us arrived, had made beds for all of us; not the ramshackle kind we had at St Omer, but superior articles with green hessian in place of the waterproof sheets.

The move down to Hesdin was a Fred Karno operation, seldom excelled even by the Artists. We had accumulated so much junk, in the form of luxuries of all kinds that we could not get our stuff into the space allotted to us in the Battalion transport. So we used the big wicker hampers provided for telephones and similar equipment, for the important things like gramophones, records and primus stoves and strung the less important official equipment on our bikes and over our own shoulders and went off looking like unmilitary Christmas trees. Several bikes were so overloaded that they broke down and their riders had to walk or cadge lifts from passing lorries. The whole journey from St Omer to Hesdin was under fifty kilometres, but it was the next morning before the last of the stragglers was gathered in.

The new barracks was much lighter and better than at St Omer, but lacked several amenities that we considered important. The first of these was electric light and we proceeded to remedy this deficiency by lowering Lance-Corporal Maris head-first out of the window – with two men hanging on to each leg – until he could tap the town supply, which ran along the back of the barracks, just under the first floor windows. Why he wasn't killed, either by being electrocuted or by being dropped on his head on the cobbles below, I do not understand. But he managed to do the job, a wire was led in, electric bulbs purchased and our two rooms were effectively lighted even before the officers had managed to get their mess supplied with electricity.

We had a very good time at Hesdin, all that spring and summer. To keep the two halves of the battalion in touch, we ran a line back from Montreuil but, as we had not enough wire to cover the whole distance, we made a terminal in a meadow by a stream about four kilometres out from Hesdin. Communication between

Artists' Rifles signal unit at Hesdin July 1916.
Back row, left to right, G.E. Cates (V.C), W. Brown, B.A.R. Shore, N.R. Clarke, B.R. Hilder, H. Retford, Reynolds, W. Withers, L.R. Mohler.
Front row, the author, W.S. Cook, Sergeant G.H. Cook, Lt. W. Margetson, Jeffries, Jack Maris, Chauncey.

the terminal and the Orderly Room at Hesdin was by bicycle. We used properly insulated D.3. wire when we could scrounge any, but the ordinary wire issued to an infantry battalion was only insulated with some sort of shellac, which tended to rub off against trees and bushes and cause faults when it rained or even when there was a heavy dew. That meant that two men from each end were almost continually patrolling to rectify faults. It would not have been much fun in winter, but it was summer and we found it very pleasant. It took one away from barracks and formal parades. And, on really hot days, there was no hardship in sitting at the Hesdin terminal with nothing on but a towel and a pair of head-phones and with a small stream at hand to dabble your feet in when you felt like it. Apart from manning the stations and patrolling the line, we spent most of our time out in the country flag-wagging to each other.

We also found a place, quite close to the town, where the Ternoise, which ran into the Canche at Hesdin, opened out into a pool deep enough to dive into. We used to go swimming there before breakfast. One wasn't supposed to leave barracks at that time, but the sentry on the gate stood with his back to the wall and, on a bicycle, one was out and down the road before he could realise what was happening.

But, after a day or two, it was reported that we were nipping out to bathe and we quite expected that the authorities would put a stop to it. What they actually did was to put a picket on the pool, which meant that some unfortunate from the companies had to get up early and watch us without being able to enjoy it himself.

Another occasion when the authorities were unaccountably lenient towards our peccadilloes was when we blew up a primus in our rooms. We were using petrol, which is not to be recommended; something went wrong and liquid petrol started squirting out on to the wooden floor. Cates lifted the blazing stove on to a dixie lid. This was very brave of him, but it wasn't really a good idea as the liquid petrol, instead of soaking into the wood of the floor, started to collect in the dixie lid underneath the burning stove.

It did not take more than a few seconds for the mixture of air and petrol to reach the right proportions for an explosion and the whole thing blew up with the hell of a bang. The windows were blown out, a mess-tin full of tea leaves went half across the parade ground and the piston-rod of the pump shot up like an arrow and stuck in the ceiling. The chaps in the room above were tumbled backwards as the floor rose under them but, possibly because most of the force of the explosion went upwards, we, who were in the same room as the stove, were more frightened than hurt. I don't know why there wasn't a row about this but, as far as I remember, we did not even have to pay for the damage.

III

Learning to be an Officer

During the summer, demands were made for more men to take commissions. Hilder refused to apply because of his stutter, which he felt would make him unable to give orders on parade, but B.A.R. Shore, Bruin, Cates and I put our names down. As far as I can remember, there was no sort of selection beyond a short interview with a brigadier, who was reputed to accept anyone who did not drop his aitches! More stringent tests were introduced later, but, even then, were nothing like as severe as the tests used in the last war, which I am sure I should never have got through.

By way of special training, men accepted for commissions were put on close order drill. Day after day we marched about under the Regimental Sergeant-Major, taking it in turns to command platoons and companies. A platoon was represented by a length of rope held by a man at each end. After weeks of this, we could, all of us, take a battalion and turn it upside down and inside out and get it back into its original formation with speed and precision, but we had no inkling of an officer's other duties.

On 30th August some of us, including B.A.R. and myself, were sent up to join the Anson Battalion of the Royal Naval Division at Bully-Grenay, near Lens. The RND were a bastard sort of body, originally created by Winston Churchill for the relief of Antwerp in the very early days of the war. They were an infantry division, largely composed of miners from Durham and Northumberland. They had trained at the Crystal Palace and not one in a hundred had ever been to sea, but they laid great stress on their naval status, many of them wearing beards to show it. Their NCOs wore army rank badges on one arm and the corresponding naval ones on the other, but only the naval designations were used. Thus, a corporal wore two stripes on one arm and crossed anchors on the other and was addressed as 'Leading Seaman'. Their sergeants were 'petty officers' and their sergeant majors 'chief petty officers' and so on. The Army tolerated this harmless idiosyncrasy and they were a good crowd though rough diamonds.

Bully-Grenay was a very quiet sector – that is why we were sent there to have our first look at the war. It was a horrible mining district, all slag-heaps and rows of dismal little cottages and a few civilians were still living within a couple of miles of the front line. We had only just taken it over from the French, which was one reason why it was so 'cushy'. The French, with their usual sound logic, believed that, if you were not going to attack, there was no point in stirring up trouble. But the British High Command would not fall in with this obvious piece of common sense and believed in cultivating what they called the 'offensive spirit'.

For example, there was a road that led up from Bully through the two front lines – ours and the Boche. At night, limbers used to bring rations and stores right up to both front lines. We could hear harness jingling and people talking in the Boche line and they could hear us and neither side interfered with the other. But some fool in the rear insisted on being offensive and ordered that the Boche transport should be shelled. The Boche naturally retaliated on our transport and the days of peace and quiet were ended, with no advantage to either side. The only result was that our ration parties had to go back and lug all the rations and stores and ammunition up on their backs through communication trenches for a mile or more. It certainly did not encourage the 'offensive spirit' amongst the troops, except against the idiots on the staff. This was the sort of thing that induced such a lot of bad feeling between the troops in the line and the staff behind it.

We were distributed amongst the various companies of the Anson battalion and, after a little wangling, B.A.R. and I found ourselves in the same company. We did ordinary duties at first and were later attached to officers as their runners. We saw a raid and went out on patrols between the lines, but the day-to-day details have been written in a diary that I kept in my F.S. book, and is reproduced at the end of this book so I will not repeat them here.

After about three weeks, we were taken out and sent back to Hesdin, where we resumed our everlasting company drill, except for one week which we spent in the Bull Ring at Camiers, near Etaples. For this, we were given the acting rank of sergeant, which I didn't enjoy. Most of the chaps in the sergeants mess were big, tough chaps, older than I was and with a good deal of experience of the war. They were quite kind but they laughed at me because I was such a baby and I felt that no one could possibly mistake me for a real sergeant, so I would have preferred not to have had to put my stripes up.

Camiers was an enormous base camp on the sand dunes where drafts were received and sorted out and various courses run. We did some elementary training and threw our first live bombs, but a week was not long enough to be any good and I, at least, did not feel in any way competent to take a commission.

Back to Hesdin and more company drill until finally, about the end of November, I should think, our commissions came through. I was gazetted as Lance-corporal Nettleton, which surprised me, as I had never held that exalted rank – not even the acting and unpaid variety – except in the corps at Rugby.

The first problem was uniform and kit. You were given a grant of £50, which had to cover such items as watch, compass, revolver, and field-glasses, as well as clothes. The trouble was to find them. People who got commissions at home could get everything in London, even if they couldn't get them in their own towns, but if you got a commission in the field, everyone behaved as though only your immediate presence at the front could save the nation from defeat. We were allowed *one* day at St Omer, where there was an officers' shop, to fit ourselves out.

So I went up to join the 2nd Rifle Brigade, with one (only) officer's tunic, a pair of ASC driver's breeches and my own private's great-coat. But I did get a very good, long-barrelled Smith & Wesson revolver and also an officer's valise, but no blankets.

With this limited equipment, B.A.R. and I set off to find our unit. I was glad he had been posted to the same battalion. We gave each other much needed moral support, but we were a pair of very innocent lambs going off to the slaughter.

Nobody was supposed to know where any unit was except the

(*Right*) The author (sitting) and B.A.R. Shore. At Bully-Grenay with the Anson Battalion, RND, August 1916.
(*Below*) Newly commissioned officers. The author is on the right of the front row and B.A.R. Shore is sitting next to him.

Railway Transport Officers. The drill was that you went to the nearest RTO and he looked up his list and gave you a railway warrant to the station nearest to your unit's listed position. But his list was always out-of-date, so the first journey was only the preliminary stage in your wanderings.

We spent all day getting to some little town behind the Somme, only to find that the RB had left that part of the line and were somewhere behind Amiens. It was dark and cold and wet and we didn't know what to do, so we appealed to the RTO. He said his duty was to dispatch bodies to where they had to go, not to act nursemaid, but he advised us to go and find the town major. We finally found this gentleman after a long tramp in the dark and the rain. He was an elderly and irascible major, who was not at all pleased at being got out of bed by two helpless and very junior officers. He told us, not very politely, that he had no billets, would never have any, and didn't give a damn where we slept or even if we slept. All he wanted us to do was to get out of his sight and stay out.

So we crept back to the station like a couple of bedraggled and frightened puppies and dossed down in our clothes on the waiting-room floor. It was a bit chilly in a valise without any blankets, but it was out of the rain and that was something.

It was not a very good beginning, but it taught us a lesson. Never again did I apply to a town major for a billet and never again did I go without one. However poor one's own efforts may be, they usually give better results than relying on someone else.

The next day we found our battalion, which was out of the the line for a reasonably long spell and were billeted in a little village, whose name I forget, somewhere behind Amiens. The 2nd RB were in the 25th Brigade, 8th Division. This was a regular division, in that all its units were regular units, but it had not formed part of the original British Expeditionary Force, because the units making it up had been scattered in India, Malta and other overseas stations when war broke out. As the units were brought home, they were gradually brought together, but the division was not constituted as a division for some time and did not come out to France till November 1914.

Because of its late start, it had a much higher proportion of

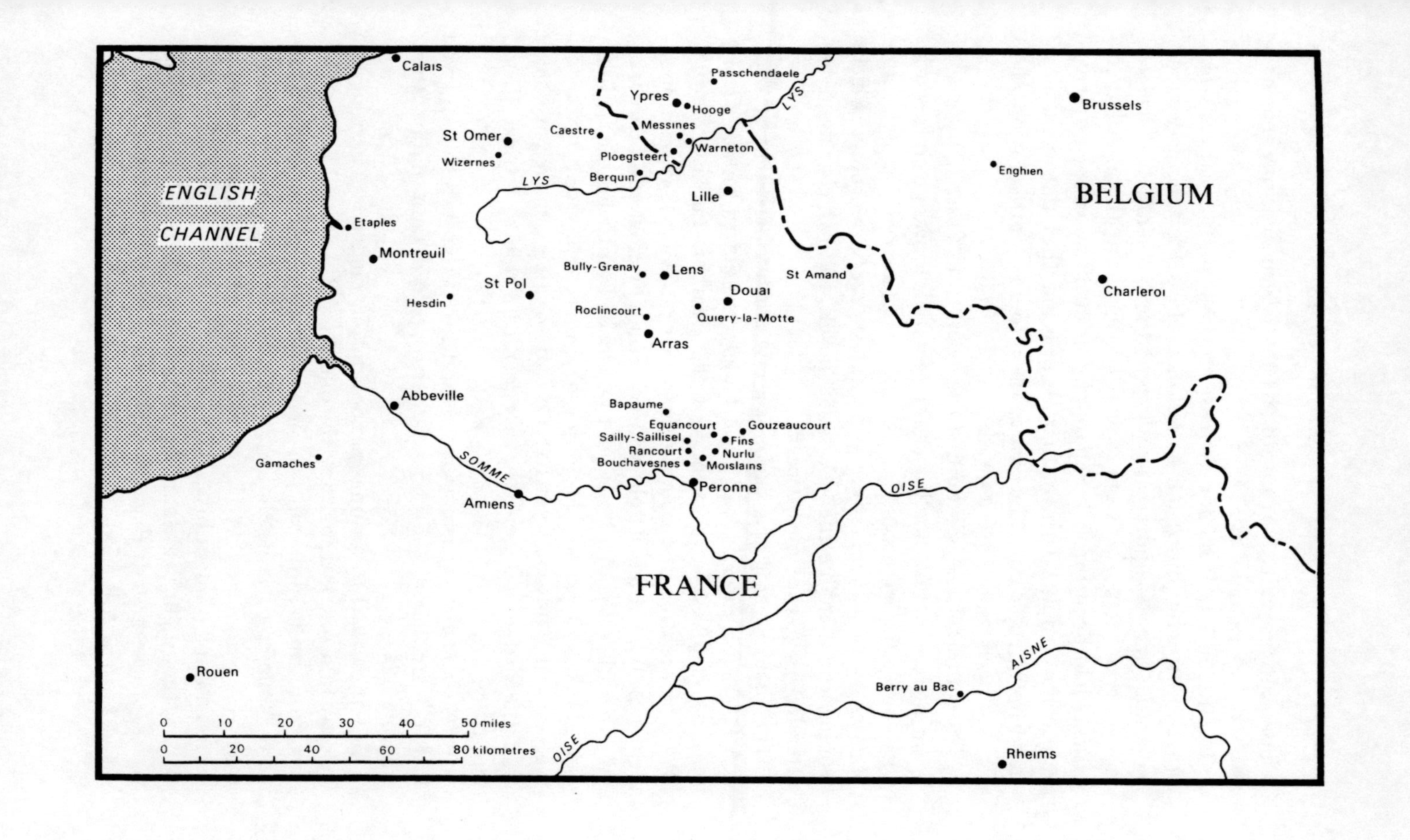

ENGLISH
CHANNEL
BELGIUM
FRANCE
Calais
Passchendaele
Ypres
Hooge
Messines
Caestre
St Omer
Wizernes
Ploegsteert
Warneton
Berquin
LYS
LYS
Lille
Brussels
Enghien
Etaples
Montreuil
Bully-Grenay
Lens
St Amand
St Pol
Douai
Charleroi
Hesdin
Roclincourt
Quiery-la-Motte
Arras
Abbeville
Bapaume
Equancourt
Gouzeaucourt
Sailly-Saillisel
Fins
Rancourt
Nurlu
Bouchavesnes
Moislains
Gamaches
SOMME
Peronne
Amiens
OISE
AISNE
Berry au Bac
Rouen
Rheims
OISE
0 10 20 30 40 50 miles
0 20 40 60 80 kilometres

regular officers left than any of the first seven divisions that had formed the original BEF.

B.A.R. and I, from the Artists, and one or two others from other units, who joined the battalion at the same time as we did, were the first 'temporary gentlemen' the battalion had had to absorb and I fear we were a bit of a shock to them. All their officers had been through Sandhurst and had had proper training before they took up their commissions and they did not understand how people could be sent to them to do an officer's job who had not been trained for it at all.

The unfortunate adjutant, Lieutenant B.C. Pascoe, bore the brunt of it. He was appalled at the material he was given to work with, but training was his pidgin and he got on with it. Battalion parades were ordered before breakfast every morning, which would be taken by the adjutant himself and which would be attended by all the new officers.

The first morning was damp and raw, with a persistent drizzle. B.A.R. and I turned up at the parade ground (a muddy field) sensibly clad, as we thought, for the weather. Luckily, we got there before the troops, because, when he saw us, Pascoe blew right up. 'Who the hell told you you could be cloaked? There was no order that the troops should be cloaked and who the hell do you think you are to turn up on parade improperly dressed?' etc. etc. The upshot was that we had to fling our trench coats over the hedge and hope that we might be able to retrieve them later.

It was another inauspicious beginning, but that was the way we had to learn things – by trial and error – in default of any other training.

But these early morning parades did, in fact, do something to help us find our feet, because the one thing B.A.R. and I could do was close order drill and our performance gave Pascoe the first faint glimmer of hope that we might not be such absolute wash-outs as we appeared. At least, we could do something, however useless a thing it might be.

But the slightly favourable impression created by our drill was soon dissipated. Because we could drill, one morning Pascoe asked both B.A.R. and me whether we would like to borrow his horse while we were showing our skill. (It is easier to drill a whole battalion from horse-back, because you can be seen and heard by everyone.) I had never even sat on a horse and refused. B.A.R. was braver – or more foolhardy. He, also, had never been on a horse, but thought that it ought not to be too difficult just to sit on one, since he would not have to try to make it go anywhere in particular at any particular pace. Anyway, as soon as he was hoisted into the saddle, the horse knew that he had a tyro on his back and started to play up. B.A.R. couldn't find the brake pedal and, in no time, the animal was galloping round the edge of the field with B.A.R. hanging round its neck with both arms.

The serious part of the business was that the horse was no ordinary officer's charger issued by the Remounts Department, but Pascoe's own private pet that he had brought into the army with him. Pascoe didn't care a hoot whether B.A.R. broke his neck or not, but he was very much concerned lest his precious animal should come to harm. The men were beginning to laugh, so Pascoe flung an order over his shoulder to me, as he started in pursuit, to move the battalion about and the last I saw of the incident was B.A.R. and the horse going through the gate of the field with Pascoe in full cry after them.

Afterwards, B.A.R. told me that the blasted horse had tried to scrape him off against every wall all down the village street and he was in fear of his life till they met the animal's own groom just by the horse lines and were brought to a stand-still. Then Pascoe caught up and, after having satisfied himself that the horse had not been damaged, rounded on B.A.R. for not saying that he could not ride and so on.

I was the next one to blot my copy-book. I am not surprised that the regular officers took a poor view of their reinforcements, because we could not be trusted to do the simplest task without making a mess of it. But I suppose it was as well that we had a few weeks in which to make our mistakes out of the line, where our errors could be forcibly pointed out to us by our superiors. It would have been much more serious if we had had to make our mistakes when we were more or less on our own, with no seniors at hand to pull us up.

Anyway, shortly after the incident with the horse, I was

ordered to take, say, 120 men (I forget the exact number) to a village some miles away for a course. We had to march to a certain place and were then taken on in lorries. We had to parade in the dark, long before anyone else was about, and when I took over the parade, the Sergeant Major reported (say) 116 men present. I asked where the missing men were, but he did not know. He suggested that some of the companies might not have been able to find their full quotas because of men on leave or sick or required for other duties. That sounded reasonable to me and, in any case, it seemed that the important thing was to get the men to the embussing point by the correct time rather than to worry why a few odd bodies had not turned up.

So off we went. We met the Brigade Major at the embussing point and when I reported myself with 116 men, he did say 'You were supposed to be bringing 120'. I couldn't explain the shortage and, in any case, it was too late to do anything about it, so we packed into the lorries and went on our way, quite happily as far as I was concerned.

About three o'clock that afternoon, I was sought out by a bicycle orderly who had ridden all the way over from the battalion, with a furious official chit from Pascoe.

> You were ordered to take 120 men on this course. It has been reported that you have only taken 116. You will explain, immediately, in writing, why you have failed to carry out your orders, who the missing men are, what has happened to them etc.

I felt pretty small and the only thing I could think of was to get hold of my Sergeant and go round the billets and check up on the missing men individually. This took some time as the men were billeted in twos and threes all over the place.

I felt smaller still when the count was finished and I found that I had had the full complement of 120 men all the time.

The Sergeant Major had either miscounted on the original parade or was trying me out to see what I would do. I had done nothing – and got into hot water about it. So, in future, I did not rely on second-hand information, even from senior NCOs, if I could check it myself.

Apart from our official misdemeanours, we were not having a very pleasant life socially. The village we were in was larger than most and we were able to get a room big enough for all the officers of the battalion to mess together. This was unusual; most of the time the officers messed in company messes, because there was seldom accommodation for more than a few to live together.

The officers mess takes a very important part in the life of a regular battalion in peace-time and is governed by a strict set of unwritten laws. These are driven into the heads of young officers before they ever join their battalions and, if they don't obey them, they are very soon brought into line by the other subalterns, by force if necessary. We didn't know anything about how to behave and were terrified of dropping bricks through ignorance.

Moreover, we lived in tremendous style, with huge parcels of luxuries from Fortnum and Masons to supplement army rations. Our first week's mess bills came to more than our pay. I know now that the other officers were living it up because one had to take any opportunity of doing so when it was offered. It was very much a case of eat, drink and be merry, for tomorrow ye die, and this was literally true for many. But we did not understand this and B.A.R. and I seriously considered applying for an exchange into another regiment. As we didn't know how to set about it we finally decided to do nothing until we had had at least one spell in the line.

One incident happened to me that did not make me feel any the less of a pariah. As part of our training, we all had to go through a gas-chamber to get used to our gas-masks. The gas-chamber was a small hut, without windows, and almost quite dark. In any case, a gas-mask cuts down your vision a great deal. We all crowded in and I found myself leaning against something that made a hissing noise. I couldn't see what it was, but it turned out to be the gas-cylinder and the outlet was pressed against the skirt of my tunic, where it left a white deposit. It was chlorine gas that they were using, which has a distinctive smell and it clung to me for days. Whenever I walked into the mess, people started sniffing and I felt like any of the 'untouchable' castes of India. But I couldn't do anything about it because I only had the one tunic, so I just had to walk about, stinking like a badger, till the smell wore off.

Altogether the first few weeks were not very pleasant. The only mild success, as far as I was concerned, had to do with my own personal comfort, and even that was due to ignorance.

As a newcomer, and a very junior one at that, I had been given a lousy billet in a tiny room that smelt abominably – even before I sat on the gas cylinder. So, remembering the incident of the town major, I set about prospecting for a better one. I found a large house, almost a chateau, and interviewed the owner, a widow, who agreed to let me have a room. I moved in and, after a day or two, mentioned it to the Assistant Adjutant, who was rather less posh and terrifying than Pascoe.

I said, 'My billet wasn't very good, so I found another one. I suppose that is all right?'

He agreed that it didn't matter but said I had better tell the Orderly Room, so that payment could be arranged. I did so, but found that I had put my foot in it again. The house I had moved into had originally been chosen as the CO's billet as it was the best house in the village. But, because the owner was a widow, with an only son away with the French Army, she could not, under the billeting laws, be compelled to accept troops. Ordinarily, civilians were compelled to give billets to troops, but exceptions were made for widows and certain other categories.

Anyway, the interpreter was summoned from Brigade to go and apologise and explain that the officer who had billeted himself on her was a young idiot, who did not know the rules, and who would be removed forthwith. But the old lady turned up trumps and said that I was no trouble and that she would be delighted to have me as her guest as long as I cared to stay. So I was allowed to remain, not without some undercurrent of feeling that it was wrong that a junior officer should have the best billet in the town, when the CO had been refused. I can only suppose that it was my baby face and frightened demeanour that did the trick.

It was a stroke of luck, but it didn't last long, because at the end of December we went into the line at Sailly-Saillsel. This was a short tour and I remember only two incidents. The first was sleeping in an elephant shelter just in front of a field-gun battery.

It was popping off right over our heads, but as soon as I got my head down, I went straight off to sleep and never heard a sound. In the morning, I found that I had been lying in a puddle of water, but not a drop had come through my trench coat. That pleased me very much; as I have said before, the British Army kit was very good stuff, at least in the early stages of the war.

The other incident was taking a large carrying party up the line with RE stores – coils of plain and barbed wire, sandbags, shovels, wire-pickets etc. We had to hand these over to a carrying party of the front line battalion on a duck-board track. It was almost impossible for two lines of men to stand side-by-side on the width of a duck-board and hand the loads from one man to the other and anything dropped just sank in the mud. When the hand-over was finished, the officer of the front line battalion's carrying party said, quite justifiably, that he didn't think he had received all the stuff that he was supposed to have received. I assured him that he had, but he would not sign a receipt for it. We argued for what seemed hours, sitting on the edge of a shell-hole and ducking down into it whenever a spray from a machine-gun came too close.

I knew quite well that some of the stuff must have been lost, but I was determined not to go back without a full receipt. I did not want to have to 'explain in writing' again why I had failed to carry out my orders. Finally, the other fellow gave in and signed to get rid of me and I went back and woke Pascoe about 2 a.m. to hand him the receipt. He explained that it wasn't really necessary to have woken him up, but he did it quite gently; I felt I had to show that I had done the job though I didn't tell him that that was why I had insisted on giving the receipt to him personally.

I was quite wrong in handling this in the way I did. It was much more important, really, that I should get my carrying party out of danger than worry about the receipt. But, luckily, this angle did not come up, because Ratliff, the other subaltern on the job, got tired of waiting for me and took the party back himself. He had been in the line before as a sergeant and knew much more about the war than I did though he was nominally second in command of the party. I always felt grateful to him for saving me from another wigging.

This incident happened on New Year's Eve and at midnight

Taken at 2nd London General Hospital. Left B.A.R. Shore, centre N.R. Clarke, right W. Brown.

there was a magnificent firework display. Both sides let off everything they had and it really was quite a sight, though I would have preferred to have seen it from further back.

After this short spell in the line, we went right back for another fortnight's rest. I do not know why we were thus favoured, but we made up for it later.

It must have been about this time that B.A.R. was wounded in an accident at a bombing school and departed almost without having seen the war. The story is worth telling as yet another instance of the folly and ignorance that does so much more harm than plain knavery. (Actual date was 19th February 1917 according to B.A.R. Shore himself).

When a Mills bomb is thrown, the handle flies off and releases a striker that is forced, by a spring, down a passage in the centre of the bomb and detonates a cap, which sets off a fuse. This fuse is supposed to burn for five seconds, before it reaches the detonator, containing fulminate of mercury, that in turn explodes the bomb. Two small holes are drilled in the cap in order to allow the products of the combustion of the five-second fuse to escape.

In this case, someone had had the brilliant idea of making one hole in the centre of the cap, instead of two, one on each edge. It may have saved a few minutes, or a fraction of a penny, in manufacture, but what the inventor did not foresee was that, when the striker was forced down, it would entirely block up the escape hole in the centre of the cap. This had the effect of converting the five-second fuse into an instantaneous one and the bomb exploded practically as soon as it left B.A.R's hand. He lost the fingers of his right hand, except for the thumb and little finger.

I suppose some people might say that he was lucky not to have suffered more damage, but B.A.R. was a musician and his hands were exceptionally important to him. But for this accident, I believe he would have become celebrated. As it was, he could play the piano with his stumps better than most people with all their fingers and he played the viola for many years with the BBC and other orchestras and made a name for himself in spite of his handicap.

I did not see him before he was evacuated, but he was my sole link with the happier world of the Artists and, after he had gone, I felt very much a stranger in a strange land.

IV

Mud, mud, mud

Towards the end of January 1917, we moved up again into the Rancourt sector – just north of Bouchavesnes – and it got very cold indeed. Patrols had to go out clad in white sheets and I remember going on a working party to dig some gun-pits with the ground frozen so hard that, when a man swung a pick, all he could chip out was a piece of frozen earth about as big as a sixpence. The frost made life easier in that it brought relief from the mud, but it made shelling very much more dangerous. When the ground is soft, a shell penetrates quite a way before it explodes and the force of the explosion is directed mostly upwards. I have had a shell drop right between me and my runner and, when we recovered, we found we were each lying on a lip of the crater but neither of us was hurt. But when the ground is frozen hard, a shell bursts on impact and the bits go out sideways and are very dangerous over a radius of a hundred yards or so.

I do not know how long this cold spell lasted, but I do remember that, when we were in huts at Maurepas Ravine, eggs and milk were frozen inside the huts. Nobody believes this story, but I am sure it is true. Part of the reason is that the Boche had a most annoying habit of sending over a few rounds of shrapnel about five o'clock every morning. I don't think they caused any casualties, but they peppered the tin roofs of the huts till they looked like colanders and any small amount of heat that might have accumulated inside leaked out through these holes.

Apart from a few days in the huts at Maurepas, we were in the line from the end of January to the middle of March, seldom getting back further than dug-outs in a quarry at Bouchavesnes, situated below the hill on the top of which ran the front line. This was reasonably safe because the quarry could only be reached by high-angle plunging fire from howitzers. Ordinary field-guns could not reach us.

But, as soon as the cold spell ended, the mud took over and became the dominating feature of one's life. Even on the track from Maurepas, up which our rations came, one calculated the speed of movement at one mile an hour and even that rate could not always be maintained. In the line itself, the mud was up to one's knees and movement was impossible, except over the top at night. There was only one small dug-out which was used as Company HQ and, for the rest, one lived and ate and slept in mud, mud, mud. Sometimes it froze and sometimes it didn't, but at all times it was wet and cold and all-pervasive. We did not get our boots off for days at a time and our clothes never. It was impossible to keep clean and we were all lousy, men and officers alike. I can still see groups of men sitting about, half-naked, in the pale spring sunshine in the Bouchavesnes quarry, picking the lice out of the seams of their shirts and squashing them between their thumb-nails.

Once, and once only, during the whole of this tour, was any attempt made to alleviate this condition by sending up a supply of clean shirts. But they were as lousy as our own, so we sent them all back, preferring to keep the lice we knew than to harbour other people's.

This sort of thing made me very angry. Someone sitting in comfort, miles back at the divisional laundry, was too slack to do his job properly and the front line troops, who were already enduring the most appalling conditions, had to suffer for it. That is the type of person who ought to have been shot, rather than some poor kid who couldn't stick the conditions and broke down.

But relations between the front-line troops and the people behind them were very bad. Nobody behind seemed to realise what conditions were like in the line. We had one man who was quite unfit, mentally and physically. He was just like an animal and had not even got the sense to take his trousers down when he needed to relieve himself. It does not require much imagination to understand that he was not a pleasant companion in the crowded conditions in which troops had to live. Three times he was sent down as mentally deficient and three times he was sent back, classified A.I. by the base doctors. We did not get rid of him till he put his trigger finger in the top of his rifle and blew it off.

Even if he was shamming all the time, he still ought to have been sent away. He was obviously no use as a fighting soldier and in conditions in which each man's morale depended so much on his comrades, he was a public danger as well as a public nuisance. No man could put up with the sort of life we were living merely through his own strength. Everybody depended on everyone else and the common stock of strength was greater than the sum of the strength of the individuals and anyone who took away from that common stock was a danger to all.

On 4th March, the division did a show. It was quite a small operation, designed to capture two lines of enemy trenches and thus advance our front line to the eastern edge of the hill from which observation could be obtained over the valley below. So good were the operation orders that, when America entered the war later, copies were sent to their staff training college as examples of how operation orders should be drawn up.

My own part in the show was a very minor one; nevertheless it was important to me as it was the first time I was given an independent command. What I had to do was to set up a prisoners collecting post just about where the Bouchavesnes High Street joined the main Bapaume-Péronne road, now part of the N37. Prisoners were brought down from the front line to this post and I had to sort them out, sending the wounded to a near-by dressing station and the others to POW cages further in the rear. Not a very difficult job, but it brought its own problems.

Zero was 5.15 a.m. and the barrage started a few minutes before this. I set out with my little party of about twenty men at 4.30 and established the post where I had been told to. It was cold, but fine, and nothing happened till the barrage started. Then we found that there was an 18-pounder field-gun battery just behind us, about a hundred yards away, and a considerable number of their shells were bursting in the air right over our heads. At first, I thought they would surely see the short bursts and do something about it, but as it went on, I went back to tell the Battery Commander that he was frightening us more than the Boche. He said he knew his shells were bursting short, but could do nothing about it. They were using American fuses, which were unreliable and which gave no indication that they were not working properly until they were actually fired. He said he did not want to kill us, but couldn't guarantee not to and advised me to evacuate the position.

I couldn't do that, because everyone had been told that there would be a collecting post at this particular point, but I did withdraw most of the men sideways out of danger leaving two men only at the proper place with orders to let me know when any prisoners started to arrive.

They started to come in within an hour or so, but not in any great quantity and were easily dealt with. They were the first Boche many of us had seen and they seemed a bit nervous, offering our men watches and money and caps as souvenirs. Our men treated them very gently and refused their offers of presents. There was only one incident, when someone from C Company came by and had an attack of hysteria, jumping about and shouting, 'Kill the buggers, kill the buggers'. But he got hold of himself when sharply reprimanded and did not actually hurt anyone.

I made one trip to the near-by dressing station, which was rather a depressing sight. The walking wounded were being sent away as soon as they had been dressed, but the more serious cases were lying about in the open, waiting for ambulances. An elderly padre was going about among them, offering cups of tea, but most of them were too far gone to take any notice and I think the padre was troubled by his ineffectiveness.

About dusk, I was told to shut up shop and go to Brigade HQ to report. I had to account for the number of prisoners received and explain what I had done with them: so many dead, so many to dressing station, so many to POW cages etc. But I couldn't make my figures balance when the Brigadier saw me and I had to ask permission to sit at a table in his dug-out and sort out all the bits of paper. I managed it in the end, but did not earn any pats on the back for my efficiency.

Just before this show, Bruin and Cates, from the Signal Section of the Artists, had joined the battalion. They were neither of them posted to my company and I had only managed to see Bruin for a few moments on the night before the show.

When I got back from Brigade HQ, I heard that Bruin had been wounded. I went to the aid-post to find out what had happened and the MO told me that a sliver of metal had cut through his eye-lid and that he could not tell me whether the sight of the eye would be lost or not. It did not sound too good and I wrote to Bruin's aunt, who had brought him up, to tell her what little I knew. Then I had some food and was sent up the line with a carrying party. I had been on the go since four that morning, but there was still a lot to do.

We had only been in support all day, the actual attack having been made by the 2nd Royal Berks on our Brigade sector, which was on the extreme right of the whole operation. They had taken two lines of Boche trenches and the position that night was as set out below: (in diagrammatic form only).

Old Boche Support – now British Front Line

A B

New Boche Front Line

Old Boche Front Line – now British Support Line

Empty

Old British Front Line

British Front Line – both Old and New

There was a block at A held by the British, and a block at B held by the Boche, but there was no communication between the old British front line and the new and it was urgent to dig a trench, as shown by the dotted line, both for communication and to form a right flank. This was done by a pioneer battalion, the 22nd Durham Light Infantry. They were mostly miners and they certainly could dig. They went down like moles; you could almost see them sinking. They had every inducement to work hard, because the Boche knew that we should be bringing up supplies and turning the captured trenches round to face the right way and so on and he plastered the whole area with shells all night long, so that it was very unhealthy to be above ground.

My carrying party went up to the old British front line and then set off for the newly captured trenches under the guidance of a man from the Royal Irish Rifles. It seemed to me that he was heading too far to the right. I questioned him several times. He insisted that he knew the way, but I got more and more nervous. I kept stopping the party and trying to listen, but there was so much shelling going on that that did not help. But I felt sure that we were walking right into the Boche lines and finally I turned the party round and went back to the old British front line from which we had started. Then I went along it to the left (north) until I came on the 22nd DLI digging the new trench. We had been much too far to the right as I suspected, but whether we had walked almost into the Boche lines as I thought we had, I don't know. Anyway, I now knew that if I kept to the left of the DLI I should be all right and had only to go due east to reach our own new front line. The so-called guide disappeared in the darkness as soon as we did our about-turn and I never saw him again.

A night or so later, I was again taking a carrying party up - we had carrying parties every night – when I met four stretcher-bearers bringing Cates down. He had been at the block A when a Boche crept up the old trench from their block at B and chucked a bomb over our barricade. The bomb sank in the mud and it would have been hopeless to try and grovel for it in the five seconds before it exploded. So Cates stood over it and told his men to get out. Most of them did, but Cates got the force of the explosion all to himself. He was groaning, but I think unconscious, when we met him. He was a heavy man and the stretcher-bearers were crying with exhaustion and absolutely done in. I lent some of mine to take him down to the aid-post, but I think he was dead before he got there. He got a posthumous VC for what he did, but his death made me feel very lonely. He had been the last of the four Artists to come up to the 2nd RB and now I was the only one left and that after only three months.

All this time I was learning very rapidly, but I never learnt to appreciate the proper regimental way of doing things. One night, just at dusk, I took a party along the main Bapaume-Péronne road towards an RE dump just beyond Bouchavesnes village. A party of the 2nd Lincolns, who had been to the dump, were coming away from it, carrying stores, and just as they turned up the road through Bouchavesnes village, they got caught by machine-gun fire. The Boche could just reach this road-junction by indirect fire, pointing their guns up in the air so that the bullets dropped down over the hill with the same sort of trajectory as a howitzer shell.

There was a ditch by the side of the road and we promptly got into it. The Lincolns scattered but had some casualties. In particular, one man who had been hit in the stomach was making a lot of noise. There was a certain amount of confusion for a few minutes and, as the dump we were making for was also under fire, I withdrew my party back towards the quarry to wait until things settled down a bit.

We were waiting near Battalion HQ, when Pascoe came out and said, 'I hope those men I saw running about down there were not your men.' I knew it was too dark for him to have seen much, so I assured him that the men he had seen had undoubtedly been the Lincolns, as we had just taken cover in orderly fashion and under complete control all the time.

But I could not understand the point of view. If you suddenly come under machine-gun fire and there is a ditch handy, surely the proper thing to do is to get into it as fast as possible. If you wait to go through parade ground movements, you just get casualties. It is true that we were walking in single file close to the ditch and could dive straight into it, but even the scattering of the Lincolns, which was so reprehensible to the regular officer, seemed sensible to me.

The Lincolns were not panicking. They did not run away, but just scattered to what shelter they could find. Then they reorganised themselves, picked up their wounded and carried on with the job. Nothing could have been more sensible. But the regular officers' training seemed to be that the men would run away if not kept under iron control all the time, which just was not true. I always found that men would obey orders and stick together under all sorts of appalling and terrifying conditions and I have seen men's lives endangered by regular officers' insistence on parade ground discipline, when parade ground discipline was not merely foolish, but downright idiotic and dangerous.

Besides, you couldn't always go by the book. You sometimes had to do things that were not in accordance with King's Regulations to save lives. I remember coming down after one spell in the line, when we were all dead tired and exhausted beyond all caring. There were only two officers with our company. The Company Commander had gone on for some reason and Moore was leading while I had the post of whipper-in at the rear. We had been plodding on for hours and were quite lost, when Moore saw a battery position and went into their dug-out to find out where we were. Everyone just slumped down in the mud and when he came out again, many of the men couldn't or wouldn't get up. I was already carrying two rifles and a Lewis gun, before we stopped, and their owners were being dragged along by the men on each side of them. It was no good threatening men in that state with King's Regulations. They did not care for court-martials or anything that the army could do to them. They just wanted to lie there and die and that is exactly what they would have done if they had been left. We had to curse and kick and drive them on by force to save their lives and I don't think any man resented it. They were too far gone at that time to resent anything anyway, but when they recovered I think they knew that what we had done had been necessary.

It is hard to make anyone who was not there realise what winter conditions were like. I saw one man die, quite peacefully and pleasantly, of nothing but exhaustion. He had been left behind when we relieved his unit. He was probably too far gone to realise that his unit had left. Our chaps found him and brought him to the Company HQ dug-out. We examined him to make sure he was not wounded and then fed him hot soup and wrapped him in a blanket, which was all we could do for him at the time. There was no possibility of getting him away before nightfall. He lay as though asleep, then started to babble, incoherently but quietly, and then just died.

Not long after Cates's death, the Boche repeated the trick of creeping up and chucking a bomb over the barricade at our trench block, but this time they did it in day-light, soon after stand-down. Theoretically, this should not have been possible; perhaps the sentry on the block was not alert – everybody tended to slack off a bit after the morning stand-to. Anyway, the bomb landed in the post and sank in the mud as before. Then it went off and wounded five of the seven men in the post.

The problem then was to get them down. The communication trench dug by the Durham Light Infantry after the show on the 4th March was still there but absolutely impassable because of the mud. The only way was over the top. It was only about fifty yards or less, but ticklish, because the block was, in effect, in the Boche front line and if it was only fifty yards from our support line, the Boche was also only fifty yards from us.

Two stretcher-bearers volunteered to try it and I went with them to provide moral support. We got up all together and ran for it and had dropped into the post probably before the Boche were aware of what was going on. But they would have plenty of time to take action while we were going back, slowly, with a wounded man on a stretcher.

Surprisingly, they did nothing. We put a man on the stretcher, hoisted him up and slowly walked back to our support line and not a shot was fired at us. Four times we did this, walking both ways now, to show that we knew that we were only doing it on sufferance and that we appreciated their allowing us to do it.

But the fifth time we started to get out of the support trench, we were met with a burst of fire. I thought that they must think we had evacuated all the wounded and were only using their forbearance to get ammunition up to the post or something. So I climbed up and hoisted the stretcher up beside me and waved a white handkerchief and did everything I could think of to try and indicate that we still had another man to fetch. But they wouldn't play any more and went on shooting and I had to give up and get back into the trench.

Thinking it over afterwards, it seemed to me that the men in the Boche line were quite willing to let us get the wounded out. But probably some officer or senior NCO came along and saw what was happening and ordered them to open fire. Even then, they behaved decently, because they could have hit me a dozen times while I was standing up waving my handkerchief at them –

in fact, they probably had to take a good deal of care to miss me at that short range.

An hour or so later, when everything was quiet again, I did manage to make a dash to the post with a blanket, but the wounded man died before dark.

Not long after this, rumours began to circulate that the Boche was contemplating a withdrawal and our battalion was ordered to make a raid to capture a prisoner. The job was given to me. I had never made a raid, but I had seen one while I was with the RND and I had no ambition to take the chief part in one.

The other officer told off for the job was a little red-headed man from Manchester, called Bowler. He really seemed to enjoy the war and went after Boche with all the excitement with which a terrier goes after rats. I have never met anyone so utterly fearless. I have seen men do incredibly brave acts, but always, it seemed to me, in spite of their fear. Bowler just didn't know what fear was. I presume he was allotted to the raid to provide the élan that I lacked and I was put in charge to put some sort of a brake on his fiery enthusiasm.

I had not had anything to do with him up to this time, but now I arranged to go out on patrol with him to spy out the land and formulate some plan for the raid. My idea was to crawl out and lie as close as we could to the enemy's wire, listen for conversation, watch for movement, try and plot his sentry posts and gaps in his wire and, generally, get any information we could. But Bowler's ideas were much more aggressive. At the first sign of movement in the Boche trench, he raised his revolver and took pot shots at what he thought was a sentry's head. That fairly raised Cain and everyone started shooting with everything they had. We just had to cower down where we were, almost touching the enemy's wire, for half an hour or more, till things quietened down a bit and we could start crawling home. After that, I decided that I would go on patrol alone every evening about nine o'clock and he was not to come out on any account until I got back again or until one o'clock, if I had not returned by then.

These patrols were singularly unpleasant, even without Bowler. The lines were so close together that you had to be on your hands and knees all the time that you were not flat on your belly. One night I stuck one hand up to the wrist in a decaying corpse. It was revolting and I thought I should never get rid of the stench. After that I always wore wiring gloves when I was crawling about in the dark. I could not fire a revolver with them on, so I carried a couple of Mills bombs, the pins of which I could get out with my teeth, if necessary. Anything was better than repeating that disgusting performance.

It was finally decided that the raid would be carried out the next time we went into the line, but just before we did go in again, the Boche withdrew and the raid was called off, to my very great relief.

This withdrawal by the Boche was not, in any sense, a rout, but an organised withdrawal to prepared positions on a shorter line. The men thought we were going straight through to Berlin, but even to those of us who knew it was not going to be quite like that, it was a tremendous tonic. The area of the Somme battlefield to which we had been confined all winter was a scene of the most utter desolation. For ten miles or more, there was nothing but a churned up sea of mud – not a leaf nor a blade of grass nor any green thing to be seen.

In the new country that we now advanced over, the Boche had taken care to destroy everything that could possibly be of any use to us. Buildings had been blown up, cross-roads cratered, wells poisoned and trees along the roads felled across them. Nevertheless, to march along hard roads, instead of ploughing through mud, to see real woods and green grass in the fields, made it seem like entering the Promised Land and everyone was in high spirits.

There was not much fighting. There were odd machine-gun nests that had to be winkled out, but it was the state of the country behind that held up our advance rather than any opposition that the Boche put up. It took some time to re-build the roads in the devastated areas behind us and until that was done, supplies of all sorts were very limited. Water was rationed to two pints a day for all purposes, which was not enough and meant that one had to shave in the dregs of a mug of tea. And food was limited to iron rations i.e. bully beef and biscuits. We sometimes used nettles as a substitute for vegetables and they were not at all bad – rather like coarse spinach.

The shortage of fresh meat led to one amusing incident. One day our Sergeant-Major saw a hare running along the sky-line and took a shot at it. To kill a running hare with a rifle would be something of a feat for even the most expert shot, but, by some fluke, the Sergeant-Major hit this one and it made a most welcome addition to the stock pot. But it fired all the troops with enthusiasm for big-game hunting and for some days they took pot-shots at anything that moved. I don't think they hit anything, but it made the countryside so dangerous that it had to be stopped.

The first night after we got out of the devastated area, we lay along a country lane. We dug small holes in the bank to put our heads in and our legs and bodies stretched out across the road. But having our heads in the ground made us feel quite safe – just like ostriches. The next night we spent in a cemetery. There was a small shrine still standing at the gateway and I allotted this to the Sergeant Major as Company HQ. His Irish batman went off calling to him, 'Sergeant-Major, Sergeant Major, I've got ye the Virgin Mary's dug-out.' For myself, I found an unused pig sty that was very welcome, as the nights were pretty cold. It was still only March.

It was about this time that we saw the cavalry in action for the first time. The History of the 8th Division had this to say:

> Next day, 21st March, the 5th Canadian Cavalry Brigade arrived on the divisional front and acted, with conspicuous success, as an advanced screen to the infantry. By skilful use of ground and cover and with bold flanking movements, often carried out at the gallop, the mounted troops ousted the enemy from positions in which he sought to stand and pressed him still more closely. On the 26th, the cavalry attacked and occupied Equancourt, subsequently handing it over to the 25th Infantry Brigade.

I wonder where the historian got that from? I was there and saw both the 'skilful use of ground' and the 'bold flanking movement, carried out at the gallop'.

Equancourt lies in a slight dip. We saw the cavalry coming up from the rear right along the sky-line. Then they divided into two troops. One troop went to each side of the village and both turned inwards and thundered down the village street towards each other. God knows what would have happened if the Boche had really been there, but, in actual fact, the village was full of our own men, lounging about in their shirt-sleeves.

I do not understand how even a cavalry-man could have thought that these were the right tactics to capture the village if it had been held by the enemy. One machine-gun or a few bombs would have turned the charge into a disorganised mob of fallen horses and dismounted men, who could have been slaughtered at leisure.

After this little bit of 'Death or Glory', there was a lull in the advance. We were not told the reason, but welcomed the rest. I and my platoon took up a position just to the left (north) of the Equancourt–Fins road. The ground rose gently to our left and the next post was out of sight beyond the rise. To the right, the ground sloped down to a high railway embankment which cut us off from everything to the south. Company Headquarters was out of sight behind us, so we were, to all appearances, entirely on our own to conduct our small part of the war as we saw fit.

The road ran straight ahead of us to the village of Fins, which was on a slight rise. The Boche had a machine-gun hidden somewhere on the near edge of the village, which commanded the road, but did not bother us. We dug ourselves a trench, spread our waterproof sheets over the top and settled down in great comfort. It is wonderful how safe you can feel in a trench with a waterproof sheet over your head. And, in fact, you are perfectly safe as long as there are no shells or trench-mortars about. The solitary machine-gun in Fins was the only sign of the enemy and that could not touch us as long as we remained in the trench.

But, of course, this idyllic existence did not last long. One morning I was ordered to take a patrol along the valley towards Fins. There was a more or less dry ditch along the bottom of the valley under the railway embankment and it was along this that we made our way. The ditch was very shallow but there was a certain amount of cover from view in the form of bushes and small trees.

Nothing happened until we had gone two or three hundred yards. Then we saw that there was a tunnel under the embankment, big enough for a man to walk through in a stooping position. I had no idea where the Boche were on the other side of the embankment and I did not like to go on with this on my flank in case somebody popped through it and cut us off. So I got up to see if there was any place where I could leave a few men to guard this tunnel and my corporal stood up beside me. We had not been out of the ditch for more than a few seconds when the machine-gun from Fins opened up and the first burst got the corporal through the head, killing him instantly.

I felt badly about this as it was my fault. I should have kept the patrol under cover and done any exploring I wanted to do on my hands and knees under the bushes. It was foolish to stand up and look about when I knew there was a machine-gun in Fins, even though I didn't know where it was.

We pulled the corporal's body into the ditch and got his papers and then tried to go forward again. But the ditch seemed to turn directly towards Fins, so that the gun would be firing right along it and we should lose even the little protection its shallow banks afforded. And we had found out the main thing we wanted to know – that the enemy were still in Fins – so I decided to go back. The Boche was, of course, wide awake now and searching for us and I had another man wounded, in the foot, before we got back to our trench.

It was the same afternoon that we met the cavalry again. They came trotting down the road from Equancourt, going towards Fins. In view of my experience on the patrol that morning, I knew damned well that they were heading for trouble, so I stood up and waved and shouted to them to stop. But they wouldn't be told. Or perhaps they thought that our shouts and excitement were the plaudits justly due from the Poor Bloody Infantry to the senior arm of the service. Anyway, on they went, about six of them under a sergeant, but within a minute they were coming back at full gallop, with the machine-gun stuttering behind to urge them on. It was lucky for them that the gun was firing straight down the road. If it had been off to one side and could have swept them from a flank, they would all have been killed.

As it was, just before they reached our trench, the rearmost horse was hit. The trooper was off before the horse hit the ground and running. The next man in front checked his horse slightly, caught the running man and swung him up behind and they were all gone in a matter of seconds.

All gone, that is, except the horse that had been hit. He got up on his fore-legs in a desperate attempt to follow, but his entrails were hanging out of his belly and he could not drag himself forward. After the excitement had died down, I went out and shot the poor brute with my revolver and the Boche made no attempt to interfere. That was the second time Fritz behaved decently towards me.

The rescue of the man whose horse had been shot was a fine bit of work, but the insensate folly of riding, in single file, up a narrow valley to an enemy position made me feel very angry. Even if they did not know that the position was occupied, they would have been wiser to scout round the flanks in open order until they found out.

I do not impugn the courage of the cavalry, but their tactics would have been out-of-date at Agincourt and they just did not seem to understand the first thing about modern warfare. We are all a bit slow in the uptake and new ideas usually have to be hammered into our heads with a mallet, but the infantry and the artillery had been learning about the new warfare for two and a half years at high pressure and it ought to have been somebody's business to pass this hardly-earned knowledge on to the cavalry, instead of sending them out raw and ignorant against machine-guns and high explosive.

V

Dessart Wood and Messines Ridge

The next event was the attack on Dessart Wood. Again I quote from the History of the 8th Division:

> The attack was opened at 4 p.m. on the 30th March, when the 2nd Rifle Brigade debouched against Dessart Wood from the northern outskirts of Fins, *which had been rushed by them at dawn.*

What actually happened was that we sent out patrols of about platoon strength every night. We wandered about in the dark till somebody said 'Boo' to us and then we came home. One night, nobody said 'Boo' and, very slowly and in great trepidation, we crept into the empty village of Fins. The truth was that the whole army had been so used to trench warfare for so long that nobody liked walking about in the open country after dark, not knowing whether the Boche was in front of you or behind you. Luckily, Fritz appeared to be as nervous as we were.

It was the same with the battle of Dessart Wood. It wasn't much of a battle, but one felt very naked and unprotected, walking about in the open.

After this there was another lull as far as we were concerned, but there was an attack on the Bois de Havrincourt by two battalions that was a text-book parade ground operation that might have been put on as a show piece at Aldershot but which one would never have expected to see in actual warfare.

Our battalion was in reserve, but I had a grandstand seat, (with no danger) because I was sent up to the HQ of one of the attacking battalions as Liaison Officer. That meant that I had no duties or responsibilities but was merely there as a messenger to go and fetch the 2nd RB if they were ever required.

The two attacking battalions assembled in a sunken road, safe from both fire and observation. This led up to a ridge of high ground, from which a perfectly open plain sloped very gently down towards the Bois de Havrincourt, two or three miles away. It was like a huge parade ground and, from the rear, one could see the whole of the battle as one can see a battle of toy soldiers spread out on a table top.

The attacking battalions marched out of the sunken road, in fours, and one went to the left and one to the right. Then they turned towards the enemy and marched straight ahead across the plain, like two worms wriggling across a plate, with perhaps half a mile between them. Behind each battalion was its CO and Adjutant, on their horses, with attendant buglers and signallers and odd bodies like myself. It was just what Napoleon must have seen as he watched his columns advancing to the attack at Waterloo.

The Boche were hidden inside Havrincourt Wood and there was no sign of them, but of course it was not very long before the attack was spotted and their field-guns opened up with shrapnel. At this, each of the battalions spread out into diamond formation, with one company in each diamond, thus:

□

□ □

□

As the gunners found the range and the fire grew hotter, each company split up into column of lumps, i.e. each company spread out into similar diamond formation, with each blob consisting of a platoon but the platoons still going forward in fours. The effect was that the plain was now covered with little blobs, each consisting of a platoon in fours, but each at a different angle and range from the guns and well separated so that no shell could damage more than one platoon. It was fascinating to watch all these parade ground manoeuvres being carried out with perfect precision and it was difficult to realise that a real battle was going on.

Soon the foremost troops found themselves within rifle range and the platoons started to open out into line and join up, in extended order, with the platoons on their right and left. Then the rear companies followed suit and you had two long lines of troops, one behind the other, stretching right across the plain and going steadily forward.

At this time, the Boche noticed the HQ groups and sent a few shells over to us, so we split up a bit. We had tended to bunch together in our interest in following the show. By now, the forward line was almost up to the wood and was lying down and firing and advancing by section rushes, still in the approved parade ground style. Then they disappeared into the wood and I went home to my tea.

The whole thing may have lasted two or three hours and was quite the best field-day I have ever seen, in peace or war. Also, it was the only chance I ever got to see a battle as a whole. Usually, one only got a worm's-eye view of a battle from the bottom of a stinking shell hole. Even when one was above ground, one's attention was less on the view than on selecting the next shell hole to dive into. This was exemplified within the next few days, when I spent about six hours with my face in the ground, as close to it as any worm.

We were supposed to secure some high ground near Gouzeaucourt, in conjunction with the 2nd Royal Berks on our left. It was very cold and there was a good deal of snow on the ground, in spite of the fact that the date was 4th April. The attack had been planned in a hurry and we (C Company) got our orders only just in time for us to get up to our jumping-off point, a sunken road, at zero hour, 2 p.m. We got out of the sunken road badly, in a bunch, and we were still trying to get the men extended into open order when the Boche machine-guns opened up on us. At first, they were well over our heads and made a not unpleasant swishing noise like angry hornets, only higher pitched. – 'Swiou, swiou, swiou.' But before we had gone more than a couple of hundred yards, the Boche brought his range down and we had to fall flat on our faces.

The first bursts caused a number of casualties, but the spot we had reached happened to be dead ground. This was accident, not design. The fold in the ground was so slight that you could not tell that it was dead ground until you had your eyes down at earth level, but it was enough to protect us as long as we lay flat. Any attempt at movement drew renewed fire and, though one man might have been able to run back and chance his luck, there was no possibility of withdrawing a whole company.

At first, we hoped that the Berkshires, who were supposed to be on our left, would come out of Dessart Wood and distract attention from us, but they never appeared and we just lay there with the snow melting under us and the wet slowly penetrating to our bellies, until it got dark enough to move. I suppose that must have been about 7.30 or 8 o'clock at that time of year. At any rate, it was the hell of a long, cold wait.

As soon as we could, we moved forward to approximately the positions we had been told to occupy. There was no sort of continuous line – just a series of posts of platoon strength at considerable distances from each other. I chose a position about half way down the reverse slope of a hill and set my platoon to digging themselves in, while I went back to find Company HQ and learn what the score was.

I found the Company Commander after a good deal of searching and got my orders. Then, on the way back to my own platoon, we (my runner and I) almost bumped into a large patrol of about fifty Germans, who were wandering about a long way behind our forward positions. Luckily, they were making so much noise that we spotted them before they could spot us. At first, I did not think they could be Boche, so far behind our lines, but we took the precaution of lying down in a ploughed field and, as soon as we got their heads against the sky-line, we could see for certain that they were Germans.

They must have passed within twenty yards of us, but we played Brer Rabbit's trick of 'layin' low and saying nuffin'' and they never knew we were there.

When we got back to the platoon, we found that they had dug in where I left them, but the Sergeant (Sergeant Leece, a policeman in civil life) said that a staff officer, whom he did not know, had found them soon after I went away and had told them to stop digging at that place and move up to the brow of the hill. Sergeant

Leece, very stoutly, said that he had been told to dig in there and he was going to stay unless he got other orders from his own officer. And it was a good job he did. All the next day, the Boche shelled the brow of the hill above us and the bottom of the valley below us and we just sat pretty in between and did not get a single casualty. That brought me a certain amount of kudos from the men, which was useful, as well as gratifying, because it increased their confidence in me and my own confidence in myself.

My recollections of the next few days are a bit hazy. They are mostly of wandering about in open country with occasional skirmishes of no great importance. At the beginning of the Boche retreat from the Somme, a new formation had been developed – the battle platoon. In this were gathered all the most aggressive spirits and they got all the nastiest jobs of winkling the enemy out of strong points etc. In our battalion, Bowler was the obvious man to command the battle platoon and he made a first-class job of it. He gathered round him an assortment of really tough rogues and they would have followed him anywhere. I remember him dashing down cellars in Gouzeaucourt without a moment's hesitation to see if there were any Boche hiding there, while I waited outside and wondered what I should do if he did not come out. I frankly hated being anywhere near him when we were mopping up a village, but he was absolutely the man for the job and earned the MC he got about ten times over.

The battle platoon was not peculiar to our battalion. Other battalions had theirs and outside Villars Guislain our battle platoon met that of the 2nd Devons in the dark and they had quite a scrap before they realised that they were not fighting the enemy.

This sort of desultory warfare continued until we got up to the Hindenburg Line, which was the prepared position to which the Boche had intended to retreat. This was a tremendously strong line, with a thick hedge of wire in front of it as broad as a main road, that could never have been taken without a planned major assault, so the British army sat down in front of it and operations degenerated into trench warfare again.

By the middle of May, we were taken out of the line and went into Corps Reserve round Nurlu and Moislains, not far from where we had started. After a fortnight there, we went north, right out of the Somme area and into the 2nd Army Reserve behind Messines. The Messines show was a great success so the reserves were not called on. For months the REs had been digging mines under Messines Ridge and filling them up with TNT. On 7th June they set them off with a bang that was alleged to have been heard in London and blew off the whole of the top of the ridge. I did not hear the noise myself. Bruin had come back to the battalion at this time. His wound had not been as serious as it might have been and his eye had not been damaged. He and I sat drinking Black Velvet - cheap champagne and French stout – until one a.m. on the morning of the Messines show and had then had to go out and walk it off because we felt sick and, when we did get to bed, we were beyond listening for bangs.

By this time, I had, more or less permanently, got the job of billeting officer, in addition to ordinary company duties. I had dropped into it more by accident than design. The first time it was wished on me was, in part, a consequence of my having found myself a particularly good billet when I first joined the battalion. The Powers-that-Be said, in effect, 'If you are so good at finding billets for yourself, see what you can do for the battalion'. I had absolutely no idea how to set about the business, but, this first time, they sent me off with the Brigade interpreter. He was very good at wheedling the old ladies and getting what he wanted by soft soap.

Under the billeting regulations, civilians could be compelled to house troops and officers, but could not be compelled to provide accommodation for officers messes – that was a matter for negotiation by the mess concerned. The interpreter would cajole the women, 'Surely in a big house like this you can find room for three officers? I will send you only '*des officiers très gentils; pas de Canadiens ou Australiens.*'

It will be gathered that Dominion troops had not got very good reputations amongst the French and Belgians who met them at the closest quarters. In fact, many of them did behave very badly and treated their hosts in a way that they would not have put up with if the positions had been reversed.

It always amazed me that the peasants and villagers were as

good to us as they were. The farms were being run entirely by the women; all the men but the very young and the very old were away with the French army. The women worked from dawn to dusk on nothing but '*de la soupe et une tartine*' and to have mobs of foreign troops quartered on them all the time only added to their heart-breaking labour. Yet they were nearly always polite and often kind and they responded immediately to small acts of courtesy and consideration such as bothering to shut the farm gates. But they knew as much about the billeting regulations as we did and it was essential to make oneself agreeable if one wanted to get anything that was not compulsory, such as a room for a mess.

Actually, it was not part of the billeting officer's job to arrange such things. His first duty was to provide essential housing for the troops. But it made a lot of difference if, after settling their men in after a long march, the officers could come in and find their own mess arranged for, instead of having to haggle about it themselves. (And when I say march, I mean march – on our own flat feet – not just a comfortable ride on a bus or lorry).

My first billeting operation went off all right, with the aid of the interpreter. It so happened that the next time any billeting had to be done, I was away on a course or not available for some reason and the man who got the job made a hash of it. I don't think it was altogether his fault, because he was as green as I was and did not have the benefit of the interpreter's aid and example. But the battalion arrived, tired and footsore, and half the companies had no billets arranged, so next time the job was wished back on me.

Well, practice makes perfect, they say, and I got so much practice that, in the end, I could be pretty confident of having the billeting completed and the officers' messes arranged for inside four hours in the average village.

Of course, this was not always possible. Sometimes the accommodation just was not there. I remember once having to hand over to the Quartermaster an empty field under several inches of mud and tell him that that was the accommodation for himself, his QM stores and his horse-lines. He cursed me up hill and down dale, but before the day was out he had got hold of several tents and organised himself a tolerable camp, while all the other Quartermasters were up at Brigade HQ, demanding his blood as a rogue and a robber.

Perhaps this is as good a place as any for a digression on the subject of Captain and Quartermaster J.H. Alldridge, MC and three Mentions in Despatches.

He had been in the Army for over thirty years and what he did not know about King's Regulations was not only not worth knowing; it just did not exist. The 2nd Rifle Brigade was, for him, the finest unit in the British, or any other, army. It was his wife and family and dearly beloved mistress and he fought for it as a lioness fights for its young. Though a normally upright and honest person, he never hesitated to perjure his immortal soul if he thought it would do the battalion any good. And he had ways and means of getting what he wanted unknown to lesser mortals. The result was that we got our rations, and even luxuries, regularly in the most impossible conditions and in spite of all that the enemy or storm and tempest could do to hinder.

One of his feats concerned the leather jerkins that we wore in the winter. (Greatcoats were impossible in the line on account of the mud.) These were ordered to be withdrawn on some date when, according to the calendar, the need for them should have been over. But the snow was still on the ground and we felt a bit sore that people sitting in warm huts miles behind the line should be so unimaginative, to put it mildly, as to insist on following the usual routine when the weather conditions were so obviously unusual. However, orders are orders and the jerkins were withdrawn from the troops and loaded into GS wagons and taken to Brigade HQ. Alldridge went with them and came away with an official receipt, shewing that he had handed in so many hundred jerkins. All this was strictly according to Hoyle, but when the GS wagons came back, it was found that, by some strange dispensation of Providence, they were still full of leather jerkins, which were promptly re-issued to the troops.

But, though he would defy the whole Army organisation in defence of his beloved battalion and do anything for you just because you were a member of the battalion, it was unwise to presume on his goodwill and fatal to try and pull a fast one on him. He regarded junior officers as unlicked cubs, who sometimes had to be disciplined for their own good. And when this happened, it was no good trying to argue with him. He knew King's Regulations backwards and forward and inside out and was absolutely sure of his ground. It was better to take your medicine with what grace you could summon up.

I have seen him throw an officer's valise off into the mud because it weighed more than the regulation 35 lbs. The owner had been unwise enough to cross swords with the QM on some other matter and, then and there, he had to jettison so much of his kit as would bring his valise down to 35 lbs.

This was pretty severe punishment, because the 35 lb limit was impossible to comply with except at the price of considerable personal discomfort. It had to cover all your belongings, including bedding, that you could not carry on your person. And that means your belongings, not for a week or a month, but for years. In my own valise I had no less than six army blankets and these alone must have weighed pretty nearly 35 lbs, but I needed every one of them during that winter of 1916/17.

But if you did not do anything to get in his bad books, Alldridge was a very good friend and I think he enjoyed playing fairy godfather to young officers. Once I lost my revolver and holster, ammunition pouch and compass, all stolen from an elephant shelter where I had left them while I went to Battalion HQ for a briefing.

I told Alldridge about it and suggested that I should report them 'destroyed by shell fire' and try to get the Government to replace them.

With a perfectly straight face, he said, 'Ah, but that wouldn't be quite honest, Nettleton, would it?'

I must say I thought this was straining at a gnat and, considering some of the camels I had known him to swallow, I was rather taken aback. However, I had to admit that it would not be strictly honest.

Then he went on 'Never mind, leave it to me and we will see what we can do.'

Some little time later, when we were in the line again, I happened to be at Battalion HQ when Alldridge came up with the rations and he tapped me on the shoulder and said, 'Go and see my batman, laddie, I think he has got something for you.' And he had, a sandbag full of replacements of everything I had lost.

I thanked him, of course, but I did not enquire where he had got them. It was generally better to accept with gratitude and not to enquire how he worked his miracles.

VI

Ypres

In the early part of June, the division went into the line astride the Menin Road, near Hooge, but I missed this tour of duty as I went home on leave, my second leave, eighteen months after my first. The only incident of note was that I lost all my kit on the way back. I had gone into the buffet at St Omer station to get some food while the train was held up there. I ate with one eye on the train and there would normally have been plenty of time to run across the tracks and catch it as soon as it started to move. But when it did start and I started after it, an enormously long goods train suddenly came between me and my train and I was cut off and left stranded with nothing but what I stood up in.

But the Devil looks after his own and a couple of days after I had rejoined the battalion, I was in the Officers Club at Toc H, in Poperinghe, when I heard some fellows laughing about the chap who had missed the train at St Omer. So I went over to them and they told me that they had not known what to do with my kit, so they had handed it over to the RTO at 'the village with the unpronounceable name'.

I knew at once what they meant by that. Many of the Flemish names were tongue twisters, but the troops usually produced some sort of an anglicised version that became current in the army, though it would not have been recognised by the natives. But Godewaersvelde defeated even the British soldier's linguistic abilities. Still, however you pronounced it, it was only about five miles away and the next day I borrowed the doctor's horse and rode over and got back all my stuff.

The reason for borrowing the doctor's horse was that it was the quietest and most amiable nag in the battalion and the only one I dared to mount. I felt ashamed of not being able to ride, but my first attempt at equestrianism had been as disastrous as

B.A.R. Shore's, though not so public. This was back on the Somme, where another young fool persuaded me to accompany him on horseback to get some supplies at a canteen a mile or so away. Because of the all-pervading mud on the roads, we cut across an aerodrome. The airmen, apparently, didn't like us doing this and one plane came and swooped at us, just over our heads, over and over again. The horses got frightened and bolted. The riders got even more frightened and flung their arms round the animals' necks and devoted their whole attention to hanging on until the horses got off the aerodrome and were brought to a halt by the mud.

Later, I made an attempt to teach myself to ride. I really ought to have asked for proper instruction, but I lacked the moral courage to do so. I waited till we were billeted in a village at the bottom of a steep valley. Then I borrowed the doctor's horse and set out by myself. Nobody could expect me to make the beast trot up the steep hill out of the village, so I walked him slowly up it till I was out of sight of everyone and then put him into a trot. It was a painful business until I learned to rise at the proper time, but I did learn eventually.

Cantering was easier, but I still was not in full control and one day the brute shied at a piece of paper that blew out of a hedge and set off at full gallop. I sat back and sawed at its mouth, but it had no effect whatever. Then I met the CO and the Adjutant, also out for a ride. I did not want them to know that I was being run away with, so I took off my cap and waved it at them, pretending that I was having a glorious gallop. I doubt if it deceived them, but the horse ran out of steam eventually and I rode him quietly home without damage and I heard no more about it. Later, when I had to ride officially, I was glad that I had put in some private practice, though I never became a skilled rider.

But this is all by the way and out of order. Soon after I got back from leave, the division was taken out of the line and moved right back to be fattened up for a big show, due to take place on 31st July. By this stage of the war, it had become the practice that when a battalion went into a big show, a nucleus of officers and specialists was always left out to make a cadre on which the battalion could be re-formed with fresh drafts afterwards. If the

CO went into the show, the second-in-command stayed out. If the Signal Officer went in, the Signal Sergeant stayed out. Similarly, in the companies, at least one officer and several NCOs were left out to make the basis of a new company. Because of this system, which was very necessary, I was left out of the show on 31st July, in case the Adjutant got killed.

In actual fact, the casualties in this operation were very heavy. No less than eight of the twelve battalion commanders were killed or wounded, including our own CO, (the Hon Roger Brand). Bruin also got wounded in this show, the first he had been in since he got back. He was shot in the forearm at close range and was out for the rest of the war, so his total time in the line could be measured in days. B.A.R. had had one tour only, I think, but perhaps not even that, before he got his hand blown off and Cates had been killed within a few days of joining us at Bouchavesnes. It seemed to me that I was already living on borrowed time.

Bruin's wound was worse than his first one had been, but the surgeons did a marvellous job on him. His arm was badly shattered and the nerves that convey impulses to the finger muscles and which, as I understand it, go round the outside of the elbow, were too badly smashed to be joined up in their normal position. So the surgeons brought these nerves round the inside of the curve of the arm and managed to make them meet by this shorter route and the only permanent damage was a slight loss of power in the last two fingers of the hand, which remained slightly bent.

I was sorry to see Bruin go, but by this time I had found my feet a bit and did not grudge him his 'blighty' or feel as desolate as I had when he got wounded the first time.

The system of keeping a number of key men out of the line was thoroughly justified by this battle. Without a substantial cadre we should never have been able to absorb the large number of reinforcements we received, especially at this time because we were in the line again in less than two weeks.

The Boche knew that another attack was in preparation and made things very hot for us, shelling the roads and tracks almost all the time. Ypres is surrounded by a number of low ridges that curve round from the north, through east, to south, like the rim of a saucer. The Germans held all the good positions on the rim and could look down and pour shells in on us crowded in the middle of the saucer. Movement of wheeled transport was almost impossible by day and the nights were made hideous by the screams of wounded and frightened horses as their drivers tried to lash them through the shell fire. I hated this, I think, as much as anything. God knows, it was bad enough for the men, but we had, in a sense, brought it on ourselves, while the horses had no part in, and could not understand, the human quarrel. They were made frantic by the smell of blood and the violent explosions and they fought like furies to escape from it all, while their equally frantic riders fought to hold them on the road and make them go forward.

This feeling of mine was not just sentimentality. The casualties amongst transport trying to get supplies up the line were so heavy that, in the ten or twelve days we were out of the line after 31st July, all the officers' chargers of infantry battalions were taken away and used as pack horses to carry up stores and ammunition. Even so, a large part of whatever was taken up in any one night was destroyed by shell fire the next day. When we went into the line on the night of 12/13th August there was still much urgency to pile up dumps in preparation for the attack on 16th August and all available troops were used on carrying parties.

This included us – C Company – because, while the battalion was holding the line along Westhoek Ridge, we were in support on Bellewarde Ridge, about three-quarters of a mile behind.

It had been a very wet summer. It rained for four days during and after the 31st July show; that was one of the reasons why the attack bogged down. But though I saw several tanks stuck in the mud, and one sunk right down so that its upper track was only just above the ground, the surface had dried a little and it was possible to move off the roads and tracks, skirting the shell holes that were still full of water, though this took an awful long time. Normally, troops moved along roads or duckboard tracks. These latter, of course, shewed up from the air like white ribbons and, whenever a new track was laid, the Boche immediately registered their guns on it. They had all the older roads and cross-roads and junctions pin-pointed already. Even miles behind the line, the roads were often under fire. As soon as one passed Vlamertinge, half-way between Poperinghe and Ypres, it was the normal practice to open out and leave a hundred yards between companies to minimise casualties if it did 'come on to shell'.

To my mind, there was something particularly nerve-racking in plodding along a duckboard track in the middle of a long file of men and hearing the Boche shelling the track a few hundred yards ahead. You couldn't stop – there were always more troops coming up behind you – and you just had to go on, praying fervently that the shelling would stop before you had to walk into it. It always made me feel as though my stomach had fallen out.

The first night after we took up our positions, the whole of C Company was detailed to carry machine-gun ammunition up to a dump and I was disgruntled to find that I was to be in charge of the party. This was not only because I knew it was going to be a very unpleasant job. It was a standing rule that, whatever the size of the unit detailed for a task, its commander went with it. If a platoon went, its commander went with it: if a company, the company commander; if a battalion, the commanding officer. Moreover, at that time, we were down to two officers only in our company, so it meant that I had to do the job alone.

I did remonstrate with the company commander as far as to say, 'Aren't you coming, then?', but he said he had been ordered to stay in the support line to be in touch, by telephone, with Battalion HQ. Though what support he could have given with the company sergeant major and a couple of signallers and the rest of the company away was not clear.

We had to go down to Brigade HQ of the 23rd Brigade to pick up the stuff we were to carry. This was situated at Birr Crossroads, where a road from Wieltje came down from the north to join the Menin Road. There was a duckboard track that led up north-east from Birr Crossroads and passed north of Bellewarde Lake and it was down this track we came. When we got to a point about half a mile from the crossroads, we saw that there was a violent 'hate' going on on the Menin Road on our left. There was pretty heavy shelling going on all over the area because the Boche knew that, as soon as it got dark, we would be moving up men and ammunition and stores by all available routes. But the shelling that we could see on the small stretch of the Menin Road near us was particularly heavy; it was a regular barrage.

The Boche is a methodical fellow and I felt quite sure that, as soon as he thought he had destroyed every living thing on that stretch of the Menin Road, he would switch that barrage on to our track. So I turned left and started across country straight towards the maelstrom and, sure enough, when we were just over half way, the barrage was switched across to the track we had just left. We suffered a couple of casualties as it passed over us, but that was nothing to what we would have had if we had stayed on the duckboard track. We struggled along until we got on to the Menin Road and then marched straight down it to Birr Crossroads. We were an hour and a half late in getting there, but we were the only carrying party from our brigade to get through at all, so the delay was justified.

The 23rd Brigade HQ was in a very elaborate dugout right under the crossroads. It was a mass of tunnels with little rooms opening off them and, though safe enough and fitted with electric light, must have been unpleasant to live in. It was soaking wet and pumps had to be kept going all the time. The Staff Captain of the 23rd Brigade, to whom I had to report, turned out to be a man who had been in Tudor House, Rugby, with me. His name was Beechmann and, at school, he had always insisted on being called 'Beckmarn' with the 'ch' hard and the 'a' long. But when I addressed him like that, he corrected me and said that he preferred to be called 'Beechman' with the 'ch' soft and the 'a' short. I dont blame him for rejecting the German pronunciation, but it was symptomatic of the times.

However, we did not stay for chit-chat, because Birr Crossroads was one of the most notorious danger spots on the Menin Road and I wanted to get my party away from it. (The other notorious spot was Hell Fire Corner, where the Ypres-Roulers railway crossed the Menin Road.)

We loaded ourselves with machine-gun ammunition in cases, which we had to carry to a dump a good way to the left of our Westhoek position. This was accomplished without any particular incident, but then there arose the problem of how to get home again.

The safest way would be to retrace our steps to Birr Crossroads and then go up along the duckboard track down which we had come. But this was going along two sides of a triangle and there was absolutely no possibility of doing it in the time available before dawn.

It must be explained that attacks almost always took place about dawn and in a battle area, such as Ypres then was, it was the practice of both sides to put down a tremendous barrage just before dawn, both on the front lines to forestall any attack and on the support trenches and lines of communication to prevent supports coming up. The weight of artillery used was enormous. Our guns were parked almost wheel to wheel and going down towards them at night, one was almost blinded by the flashes in one's eyes. The Boche, having their guns round the outside of the perimeter, could mass even more of them to pour shells into the interior of the Salient. It was officially reported in the US *Infantry Journal* that on the one day of 31st July British artillery fired 23,000 tons of ammunition. I have no figures for the Germans, but they must have at least equalled this total, if they did not exceed it. And all this was concentrated in a comparatively small area. So it will be understood that I was anxious not to be caught in the open when the dawn barrage came down.

The only thing to do was to try a cross-country march along, so to speak, the third side of the triangle. The good points were that I knew where I was and I knew where the trench was that I was trying to get to. In Richmond Park, it might have made a nice little problem in compass marching by night. But here, a derelict tank or an old gun could throw your compass out without your knowing it; when you decided on a bearing, you couldn't take two steps in a straight line, because you had to be weaving round shell holes all the time; and we were trying to hit our trench end on, so you could easily pass within a few yards of it in the dark and not see it.

Altogether, things didn't look too hopeful, but we followed the required drill, sending out two men as markers, lining them up on what I hoped was the correct bearing and marching up to them and then repeating the process. But it was slow work.

To make matters worse, we hadn't gone very far when we came across a mass of wire, that we could not get through. I don't know what it was – perhaps the remains of an old redoubt or something. As we could not get through it, we had to go round it, which meant going so many paces at right angles to our original direction till we came to its flank. Then we had to go along the flank on our original bearing and back along the other side for so many paces, hoping to arrive at the spot where we should have been if we had been able to go straight through the obstacle.

I was going through the motions according to the text-book, but I had no faith in what I was doing. Once I found myself right alongside a tank and at least once I found myself taking bearings with my tin hat on. I might have been doing it a dozen times for all I knew before I realised that it was silly. In addition, I kept looking at my watch and the hour beyond which we could not afford to be caught in the open was getting desperately close. We seemed to have been plodding on for hours; I had no idea where we were and was afraid that we must have missed our trench altogether.

I was just about ready to panic when we came to a small hollow and I called a halt, ostensibly to give the men a rest, but really to give myself time to think.

The place where we stopped seemed sheltered so I allowed one match to be lit for a cigarette and every one else lit theirs from this one. I also sent out a corporal and two men to scout round in a semi-circle in front, like hounds making a cast, to see if they could find any known land-mark, though this was only a last resort and I did not really hope for anything to come from it.

But I had not finished my cigarette when the corporal came back and said he had found our trench. I was never so glad of a miracle in my life; because it was a miracle. To hit a trench, end on, over that country and that distance, at night, was not something that could have been achieved by compass navigation by the most skilled navigator. It was luck, Providence, a miracle, call it what you like. I made no attempt to explain it – I just gave thanks.

We filed into the trench and I reported to my Company Commander. I must admit that I took a certain amount of pleasure in finding him in a bad state of wind-up. He would have been in the unenviable position, if we had not got home, of losing his whole company in one go.

Incidentally, I found out later that the hollow where we had stopped, Zeal House, was a favourite target of the enemy – he shelled it about every half hour, day and night. We must have hit one of the lulls, but it was lucky that we only stayed there about ten minutes.

And we had got home only just in time. Within a quarter of an hour of our arrival, the dawn barrage started and tons and tons of metal came hurtling down on us. The earth shook and you couldn't distinguish individual explosions. You could only cower in the bottom of the trench like a frightened animal, too numbed even to think.

This all-night carrying party must have been on the night of 13/14th August. The next day I was sent for by Battalion HQ and told that I was to be responsible for getting the 2nd Royal Berks up to their jumping off position on the night of 15/16th August to do an attack at 4.45 am. on the 16th. They were to be on the right flank of our division and the route to be followed led up the duckboard track from Birr Crossroads to Bellewarde Ridge. Then we had to turn south along the ridge for about half a mile and then east down into the shallow valley and up to the top of Westhoek Ridge for perhaps threequarters of a mile. Not, on paper, a very difficult march, but it had to be done in the dark and there were no landmarks whatever except the contours of the ground and the ground itself, of course, was all pitted with shell holes that were full of water.

I was promised every assistance, but, as so often happens in war, everything went wrong and all the safety precautions failed. The official history says:

> Owing to the darkness of the night and the broken nature of the ground, the attacking troops on both brigade fronts found it no easy matter to make their way up to the assembly positions; despite the fact that guides had reconnoitred the way both by day and by night and that small posts or tapes had been laid out by the Royal Engineers to assist in keeping direction. This difficult task had been admirably executed – by the 490th Company RE on the 25th Brigade front.

In actual fact, no tapes or posts at all were laid out on our route. I tried to get flags to put up myself, but, though they were promised, none arrived.

As a further help, I arranged for men to be stationed with red-light torches in two places on the reverse slopes of Westhoek Ridge – one group approximately opposite where we expected to come out on top of Bellewarde Ridge and one further south, where we had to turn east to cross the valley preparatory to climbing Westhoek Ridge.

These groups were instructed to flash their torches continuously from 11 p.m. till we arrived. I hoped to pick up the flashes from the first group as I came out on to Bellewarde Ridge and that would tell me to turn south. Then I intended to go south until I was opposite the second group and at that point I would know I had to turn east. But we had a sticky time coming up from Birr Crossroads and were much later than we expected and both groups had got tired and given up their torch-flashing before we were in position to see them, so we got no help from them.

As guides, I got 16 men – one for each individual platoon of the attacking battalion. I reconnoitred the route myself first, and then I took my little party over it again and again. I don't know how often we made the trip, but we seemed to be traipsing up and down along it all day and all night. When we finally went down to Birr Crossroads to meet the 2nd Berks soon after dark on the 15th, I felt confident that I knew the route, but very doubtful about the rest of my party. I told the CO of the 2nd Berks that it was of the utmost importance that every man should keep in touch with the man in front of him, and he impressed it on his officers, but it was a counsel of perfection that it was impossible to carry out. Even at home, in peace-time conditions, troops moving across country in single file in the dark almost always lose touch. Here, with the broken ground and under shell fire most of the time, keeping touch was an impossibility. The delay caused by one casualty, or even by men ducking and falling about when a shell comes near, is enough to break the line and once it is broken it is extremely difficult to catch up. The slightest check is cumulative and, even on a road, the back of a column can be running and still be being left behind. And here you couldn't run even if you wanted to.

We knew all this, of course, and went dead slow in front, with frequent pauses, but when we finally got up on to Westhoek Ridge, we found that we only had one company with us. The CO was naturally furious and I went back to find the missing sheep; partly to escape his wrath and partly because I was pretty sure that my platoon guides were useless and that, if I didn't find the troops, they would never get up to their positions.

To cut a long story short, I did finally succeed in rounding up the missing companies, but it took all night and they reached the jumping-off line only twenty minutes or so before zero hour, 4.45 a.m. In fact, I was still on my way to Battalion HQ to report when our barrage opened, to be followed immediately by the Boche reply.

When I did reach Battalion HQ, I found them all very much shaken. They were in a house that the Boche had concreted to make a pill-box. About half an hour before I got there, a stray shell had come in at the door-way and burst just inside, killing a young regular officer who had just joined us and who was acting as adjutant. It had not only killed him but plastered him all over the place. Everybody was in a bad state of shock both from the blast and from the horror of having this boy spattered all over them.

This was, of course, part of the penalty of using captured Boche pill-boxes, though there was nothing else to use. The thinner rear wall and the entrances at what had been the back of the pill-box were now in the front as far as we were concerned and a direct hit was much more damaging than it would have been on the solid front.

This was a bad beginning to a bad day – one of the worst, in my memory, as far as the actual fighting was concerned. Our attacking battalions took their first objective and, in some places, reached their second, but the division on our right could make no progress at all, so our forward troops were soon being enfiladed by machine-gun fire from the right. Then the division on our left, which had gone forward with us was driven right back to its starting point, so we were left in a completely untenable position, with both flanks exposed. Companies of the RB were pushed in here and there to try and stabilise the position, but could only delay matters a little. By 9 a.m. the Irish Rifles had not a single officer left and the 2nd Berks were in little better case. At one time, even the Brigade HQ personnel were pushed into the line. The Brigadier (Brigadier-General C. Coffin) was here, there and everywhere (he got a VC for his part in this show) but the whole situation was very confused, with enfilade fire from both flanks, continual counter-attacks and units all mixed up.

My own recollections are a bit hazy. I was kept at Battalion HQ for some time, probably to replace the adjutant who had been killed. I do not remember doing anything much, but I do remember five signallers being sent out, one after the other, to try and mend a broken telephone line. There was the hell of a barrage going on and none of the five got more than a hundred yards or so from the pill-box. The second man was killed just outside it, so that the rest had to step in or over what was left of him and had no excuse for not realising what they were going into, even if they had been unable to hear the din. Yet no man hesitated to go. Finally, there was only the CO, the Signal Officer (Pinnock), the telephone operator and myself left. When the fifth man did not come back, Pinnock took up his tin hat and, without saying a word, went out to do the job. I think he must have been glad when he could legitimately go himself, because it was pretty horrible for him to have to sit there and send his men out, one after the other to almost certain death. The CO was all white and strained, wondering whether he ought to stop the butchery. It must have been almost impossible not to say the word that would have stopped the men going out, but he had to think for the battalion and it was vitally important to get in touch with Brigade.

I say 'the word that would have stopped the men going out'. No verbal orders were given to them to go. Pinnock just looked at each man and each man went as his turn came. As far as I remember, no words were spoken at all until we heard the operator speaking into his telephone. Then he turned and said 'Through to Brigade, Sir', and that broke the spell.

My bones were turned to water, because I had the technical knowledge to do the job and was wondering if I should be sent out if the Signal Officer did not succeed in finding and repairing the fault.

I was frightened to death of going out, but still more frightened that, if I did get ordered, I should not be able to make my legs carry me to the door.

Sometime later, I have no idea whether it was morning or afternoon, there was some discussion as to whether the one remaining company (C Company) should be moved forward. It was finally decided to move and I was sent out to warn them. But, before I had found the Company Commander, the CO started ahead himself, waving his stick for us to follow. We only went about two hundred yards and crowded into a partially dug trench, which was a very bad place to be. The CO went away to the left to try and find out what was happening. I was very unhappy about our position. The trench was only about shoulder-deep, with no bays or fire-step, and we were crowded in two deep. If we had been attacked, half the men would have been unable to fire and the congestion could only serve to increase casualties.

The Company Commander had taken up a position behind a pill-box on our right front and I went over and asked him if we could not send some of the men either backward or forward to find a more sheltered position. But he insisted that we should stick it out where we were.

All this time we were being very heavily shelled and one field-gun battery, in particular, had us absolutely taped. Their shells were bursting just behind us and you could feel them practically parting your hair as they whizzed over. I knew, with absolute certainty, that sooner or later one would fall a little short and catch us. It did – and burst right in my face, killing the man behind me and the men on each side. I was saved by the trench being blown in on top of me.

I remember thinking, 'This is it' and then I didn't know any more until I was dug out. I was bleeding from the nose and I thought also from the ears, though I do not know how one could bleed from the ears without having them damaged, so that may have been just imagination. Anyway, I was very shaken and I went over to the Company Commander and asked permission to go to the Battalion Aid-Post. I remember being very angry with him because he would not give me leave nor withhold it. I wanted him to make the decision, but all he would say was, 'If you feel you have to', which left the decision with me. But I did feel I was justified in going, so I went.

The medical sergeant at the aid post gave me some brown stuff out of a mug and told me to lie down. Ten seconds afterwards, though he said it was two hours, he woke me up and said my place was needed for more casualties*, so I got up and went back to the company. I remember running like a hare and dodging about to avoid shells, which was absurd. You might as well try to dodge the rain-drops in a thunder-storm. But I also remember seeing two stretcher-bearers knocked over three times by shells near them in less than that number of minutes. Yet they picked themselves and their burden up and plodded steadily on as though they were just carrying something down a quiet country lane. When I did get back to the company, however, I got a great welcome from the men who said they quite thought I had gone for good.

Later, the aid post sergeant told me that what he had given me to drink was about half a pint of neat rum, but it had no more effect on me than a drink of milk.

* In later correspondence the author recalls that, probably on this occasion, when the battalion was relieved after three days in the line is was reduced to one officer (the author) and about 60 men. (The full establishment for a battalion then was about 1000 all ranks.)

VII

Plugstreet

My history book tells me that we remained on Westhoek Ridge all the next day and night, but I cannot remember anything about it until after we had been relieved and were coming out of the line. For some reason, I was not with the company, but was coming down alone with my runner and we were going across country to avoid the Menin Road, which was always a good place to stay away from. We had got a long way towards Ypres, well out of field gun range, when the Boche started sending 8-inch shrapnel shells which burst right over our heads. A shrapnel shell that bursts right overhead is not very dangerous, because the shrapnel is sprayed forward and covers a cone-shaped area about two hundred yards long in front of you. The only real danger is from the base-plate of the shell which tends to be blown backward. But the crump of these heavy shells right on top of us was very alarming and it felt as though they were intended for us personally as there was no one else in sight. And one was always more windy coming down the line than going in. The nearer you were to safety, the worse luck it seemed to be hit.

And when you were going on leave, it was worse still. Men who stood up to all sorts of horrors in the line, behaved like frightened rabbits when they were going on leave. It was a well-understood phenomenon and nobody thought the worse of you for it.

I do not know what our casualties were in the two shows of 31st July and 16th August, but they were very heavy. The Divisional History says that when we were inspected by Sir Douglas Haig on 21st August near Caestre, there were less than 4,000 men on parade. The normal peace-time infantry establishment of a division was about 12,000 men, and though we were not up to that strength when we went into the line, we were now obviously no more use as a fighting unit. Although I had been with the battalion only nine months, I was already almost the oldest inhabitant and certainly the oldest surviving officer except for the QM. The average life of an infantry subaltern was reckoned as being three months, so I had already had a lot more than my share of luck.

I now took on the job of adjutant. I was a very bad one, because I had no idea how to do the job and had to learn it, as I had had to learn all the other jobs, by trial and error. I was so bad that, whenever a Sandhurst trained regular officer came out to us, he was made adjutant instead of me, but the replacements got killed and I went on, so I kept getting the job back, simply because there was no one else to do it. In fact, I was kept at Battalion HQ as general dogsbody and emergency man, with the nominal title of Intelligence Officer and did not go back to company duty until after the armistice.

We had about a week's rest in the Caestre area and were then sent into the line near Ploegsteert (Plugstreet to the troops). This was a quiet sector and we were sent there to give us time to recover and assimilate drafts and generally reorganise. The right of the divisional area was covered by the river Lys that ran between our front line and that of the Germans. This was held all the two months or so that we were there by the 23rd Brigade. The less comfortable northern sector was held by the 24th and 25th Brigades alternately, so that we did get regular spells out of the line.

Even on the northern sector the Boche lines were nearly a mile away from ours and there was none of that crawling about on your belly that we had had at Bouchavesnes. Moreover for Battalion HQ we had a really deep dug-out with wire bunks and, above ground, a little room cut in the side of the trench, with a tin and sand-bag roof on it, in which we used to eat our meals. And there was not the continuous shelling of the whole area that made life so unpleasant in the Salient. The Boche used to shell our HQ with heavy 8-inch stuff sometimes, which shook the whole dug-out and put out the candles, but was only a minor irritation.

While all this should have been very pleasant, I developed a bad case of 'dugoutitis'. I suppose it was delayed reaction to the strain of Ypres and in modern jargon would be called 'combat fatigue', but we did not know the expression then. Anyway, the effect was that I just wanted to hide down in the dug-out all day and all night like a troglodyte. I never went out into the open unless I was sent or forced myself to go and I had great difficulty in forcing myself. I lost any desire to do anything that I did not have to do and only recovered very slowly.

Although this was a quiet sector, there was a certain amount of activity in support of the major operations that were still going on further north. One of these was a gas attack by means of Livens projectors. These were cylinders of gas that were dug into holes in the ground with an explosive charge at the bottom and some hundreds of these were put in by the REs. At a prearranged time they were all set off and the cylinders themselves were shot over into the Boche lines on to chosen targets. This was an improvement on the old form of gas attack in which the gas was released in our lines and allowed to drift over to the Boche. In the first place, you did not have to wait for a favourable wind. In the second place, the cylinders only burst and released the gas on the target, so the greatest concentration of gas was actually on the target and, even if the wind was unfavourable, the gas had largely dispersed by the time it drifted back to our own lines.

Another show was an elaborate set-piece to make the enemy think that an attack in front of Ypres was to be extended right down to our position. A great deal of false activity was put on in the back areas. Unnecessary trains were run up to the rail-heads behind us; troops were marched about the roads in daylight and a number of dummy tent-camps and dumps were set up. These were garrisoned by half a dozen men with orders to make play with Lewis guns whenever a Boche plane came over. They were also furnished with bundles of straw to simulate fires if a bomb was dropped near a dump or camp, to make the Boche think that his planes were doing a lot of damage.

In the line itself, we were supplied with a number of dummy figures that were laid on the ground in front of the front line and that could be raised by pulling a wire. At the time the attack up north was due to start, we sent over a lot of smoke and then pulled the dummies upright in the hope that the Boche, seeing them through the thinning smoke, would think that they were troops coming over the top. At the same time, the artillery put down a barrage as they would have done if it had been a real attack. Apparently, the scheme had some success, because the Boche replied with both artillery and machine-gun fire and reported that a British attack had been repulsed. Our troops entered into the spirit of the thing and treated it as a huge joke.

We had one unusual advantage here in that we held the higher ground and could see everything that was going on in the Boche lines. Everywhere else, it had always seemed that the Boche had the advantage of the ground and that we were the ones that were being looked down on, both literally and metaphorically.

Because of these conditions, my Intelligence Section did a good deal of sniping and observation. I was sent down to the camouflage school, near Boulogne, for a couple of days to learn something about it. This was an amusing place, manned largely by Chinese. As you walked about, grinning Chinks would pop out of unsuspected holes in the ground or from dummy trees and they loved doing it. It was like playing hide-and-seek with kids.

I brought back with me a dummy tree stump which we set up on the hill above Plugstreet chateau as an observation post for the gunners and a box observation post for our own front line. We had to take down the old tree stump on Plugstreet hill and put up the hollow replica in its place all in one night, so that the Boche would not know that anything had been changed and it was a great success. This hill was a wonderful observation point; so good that it attracted too many sightseers, which annoyed the gunners, because the sightseers attracted shells if they were not careful. But I was allowed up there and saw some good shoots.

The observation post for our front line was a sort of box,fitted with curtains over the door and over the loophole, and this also had to be dug in in one night. We could see the enemy's Battalion HQ and watch everyone who went in or out. Later, we set up a snipers' post in No Man's Land that could fire right into their front door and managed to annoy them considerably.

On their side, the enemy used a tall factory chimney in Warneton as an observation post and our gunners spent their spare time in trying to knock it down. It must have been made pretty well solid inside with concrete, because field-gun shells merely seemed to bounce off it and even shoots with 8-inch howitzers never succeeded in demolishing it.

One impudent trick by the Boche that annoyed us was the sending of a patrol across the Lys on our extreme right, where the line, because of the protection afforded by the river, was only lightly held by small posts at some distance from each other. The Boche patrol lay in wait between two posts and snaffled our postman, who was taking letters round to the companies in the line. I should not think they can have got much information from the letters they captured, but our CO (Roger Brand, who had returned after being wounded at Ypres) swore that he was not going to be kidnapped like that and, when he went round the line at night, took a bodyguard of six stout fellows with him.

I was impressed by something I found out here about our second-in-command, Major J.J.B. Cole. I was coming back with him, in daylight, from a trip round the line, when the Boche started dropping gas shells on an open field that we had to cross. It was not a proper attack to saturate an area, but just one battery dropping salvos of six shells at intervals, hoping to catch anything that might be moving about.

We saw what was happening when we were still four or five hundred yards away; you could tell that they were gas shells by the gentle 'plop' with which they went off, quite different from the explosion of an ordinary whizz-bang. Major Cole said to me, 'If they do that while we are crossing, put your gas-mask on as quickly as you can and then give me a hand with mine, will you?'

That astonished me and it came out that, because of a previous wound, he could not raise his arms high enough to put his own gas-mask on. That struck me as being brave far beyond the call of duty.

The general attitude, as I saw it, was that you had to carry on as long as you were fit, however much you disliked it, but that if you got a legitimate excuse for getting out of it, there was no shame or dishonour in welcoming it with open arms. To pull strings, as he must have done, to get back to the line before he had to was something the ordinary man could not be expected to do. For myself, nothing in the world would have induced me to come back to France with the knowledge that I couldn't put my gas-mask on, if I needed to.

This Major Cole was the brother of the great practical joker who originated the stunt of dressing up as workmen and digging an unauthorised hole in a road and who was always doing things of that sort. Major Cole used to tell most entertaining stories of his brother's exploits; in particular about how he inspected units of the Home Fleet at Portland in the guise of the Sultan of Zanzibar.

It was while in this sector that I had my first personal encounter with the Boche at close quarters. On 23rd September I was going round the line at night with the subaltern in charge of that particular part of it, when one of the sentries spotted us and said he thought he had seen something move out in front. The subaltern said, 'Well, shoot, you fool, and challenge afterwards' and at the same time climbed on to the fire-step and fitted a cartridge into his Verey pistol. I had just got up beside him when a number of figures suddenly rose from inside our wire and made a rush at us.

The subaltern fired his Verey pistol at the figures, instead of into the air, and the Verey light hit one of them in the eye or on the forehead, and stuck there, fizzing. By its light I saw an enormous Boche, ten foot high and weighing about two hundred and fifty pounds, or so it seemed, coming at me. I fired blindly and the man dropped like a log. I remember thinking, in that instant, how glad I was that I had a .45 revolver and not one of the little automatics that were then becoming very popular. A small calibre automatic would have killed him all right, but would not have stopped him dead in his tracks as the heavy .45 bullet did. He would probably have continued to go forward with the impetus of his own rush and knocked me down into the bottom of the trench.

There were then a few hectic minutes of general confusion and a lot of noise, but the Boche were driven off leaving two *Unteroffiziers* and five other ranks dead. They did not get a prisoner, which is presumably what they were after, and we had no casualties.

This raid had an interesting sequel and our CO got into hot

water over it; it requires a little technical explanation.

The field telephones issued to infantry battalions were comparatively simple instruments. The current went out along a wire and the circuit was completed back through the earth, the earthing being completed by a metal spike thrust into the ground or when the ground was wet, as it always was in Flanders, by a metal plate in the base of the instrument itself. Soon after both sides had settled down in trenches, it was found that the enemy were picking up our messages. We tried to stop it by using two wires, thus eliminating the return through the earth, but still the Boche could overhear all that was going on. So an instrument called a Fullerphone was produced, which worked on the principle of sending out only a very small current along the wire. This was not strong enough to operate the buzzer at the other end, but it was strong enough to open a valve and let current from the receiving machine operate its buzzer. (A child cannot move a steam engine, but it can open the regulator to let the engine's own steam into its cylinders.) This was successful, but only for the buzzer circuit. If the telephone circuit was used, the benefit of secrecy was lost. Therefore, the use of the telephone in the line was barred except in major emergencies.

When the Boche raided us, Battalion HQ could hear that something was going on, but no one knew exactly what. Even the Company Commander of the company concerned did not know for some time. The CO was frantic for information and started using the Fullerphone telephone circuit illegally to talk to people in the front line. Entirely unknown to us, there was an Army detecting station almost under our Battalion HQ and they took down every word of the CO's conversations and reported them to the higher command. The next day the CO was called to Divisional HQ and it was all read out to him . . . He had tried to disguise his questions and wrap up his meanings while talking, but when all the conversations had been analysed, it was shown that he had given away all the code names of the posts in the line and their positions. The Boche could have deduced pretty nearly all our front line dispositions from these apparently innocent conversations. It was a most interesting example of intelligence work, but our CO got a dressing-down.

I think it was bad luck on him though. After all, he had to find out what was going on. He was not to know it was just a raid. It might have been a serious attack and he would have had to make dispositions to counter it.

VIII

Passchendaele

About the middle of October, rumours began to circulate that we were to be sent to Italy and we all got very excited at the possibility of getting away from Flanders and its everlasting rain and mud. But this was too good to be true, and we were not really surprised when we learnt that we were bound for a rather less pleasant destination – Passchendaele.

We were relieved by an Australian division about 10th November ber and moved back to the Berquin–La Motte area, south-east of Hazebrouck and just north of the Forest de Nieppe. On 16th November our (25th) brigade moved up to take over the line from the Canadians who had, only ten days before, taken Passchendaele Ridge. This was the outermost of the several ridges that surrounded the 'saucer' of Ypres and marked the limit of our advance after a whole summer's fighting, of which our shows of 31st July and 16th August had been part.

The continuous fighting and the wet weather had combined to make the ground conditions simply appalling; worse, even, than they had been on the Somme. The various ridges round Ypres naturally drained down into the valleys between them and the water was normally carried away by small streams at the bottom of each valley. But the continual shelling had destroyed all the natural drainage systems and each little stream was now just a marshy area. Movement was impossible except along corduroy roads or duckboard tracks. If a man slipped off a track, it was unlikely that he could extricate himself from the mud by his own efforts and sometimes even his mates could not rescue him. Guns sank in the mud till they were unusable and sometimes sank right down out of sight into it. There was no shelter in the line except for captured pill-boxes and it was impossible to dig trenches. The best one could do was to link up adjacent shell holes to make a slight shelter for a group of men.

Even well behind the lines conditions were very uncomfortable. When we were in the line at Passchendaele, our supporting brigade was as far back as Wieltje and even there there were only rough huts made of elephant shelters or in one case, at Capricorn, tents. These had a sand-bag wall built round the outside of each tent to a height of about 2ft 6ins, which was sufficient to stop splinters, but one felt very vulnerable under shell fire in a tent.

And from these support areas to the line was a long journey – perhaps only five miles in distance, but a relief would take a whole night and a long winter's night at that.

On the 16th November we started our move into the line and got as far as Ypres for the first night, which we spent in dug-outs on the ramparts. Last time I went back there, I could still identify the place. Then we moved up into the line the next night, 17th/18th November.

I hated that journey up – worse and worse every time I made it. There was one place, on the Gravenstafel Ridge, that seemed to me to be the worst place in the whole Salient. It was completely exposed and when you looked about, the circle of Verey lights which marked the line seemed to go right round behind you and you felt entirely surrounded and trapped. And every time we passed this place, whether going in or out, there always seemed to be a fresh mess of smashed limbers and disembowelled mules through which we had to pick our way.

Nothing in particular happened on this tour, but we only stayed in the line a couple of days, being relieved on the night of 19/20th November. That in itself is an indication of what conditions were like. Reliefs were hazardous operations and they would not have taken place every other night if it had not been absolutely necessary. But two days at Passchendaele in winter was enough for the most earnest seeker after austerity and a great deal too much for most men. However, we only had one brigade front to hold, so if each brigade held it for two days, that meant that you had two days in the line and four out.

Even on your four days out, it wasn't all beer and skittles. The accommodation was, as I have said, pretty primitive, but you did at least have some shelter from the weather and could get hot food. But most of the camps were within the reach of long range guns and there was a good deal of persistent, though not continuous shelling. I remember that one evening half a dozen of us were sitting round a brazier after dinner when a shell came through the roof of the shelter, through the brazier and into the earth floor – and failed to explode.

The worst of the minor horrors were the everlasting RE fatigues. You would get a good hot dinner inside you and sit round a brazier, enjoying the blissful feeling of being warm and dry and it seemed that earth had nothing better to offer. Then, at a certain time, you had to struggle into your kit and go out into the rain and mud and take over a party of miserable-looking individuals draped in their water-proof sheets. You tramped off to some rendezvous with an RE NCO, with nothing to look forward to but hours of digging a hole in the ground or carrying impossible loads to places that didn't exist. And the drizzle began to penetrate, the first cold drops found their way down your neck, water seeped through your puttees and boots and you stumbled through the dark and cursed and swore and wondered why you ever left your happy home. It was almost worse than being wet and miserable all the time as you were in the line.

But we had not been brought up merely to hold the line. Incredible as it may sound, we were expected to do an attack and the planning of this attack was a classic instance of how completely the staff were out of touch with conditions in the line.

They say that later, when he saw the ground over which he had sent troops forward, Haig wept. I hope it is true. He certainly had something to weep over. I don't mean that Haig should have paddled round the front line himself; that was not his job. But he ought to have kept himself informed of the conditions by sending some of his staff officers up to see things for themselves, even if this did mean their getting their lovely shiny top-boots dirty. Not once in the Salient did I ever see any staff officer of a formation higher than brigade within miles of the line, nor did I ever hear of anyone who did.

This sharp division between the staff and the front line troops was very bad for morale. The troops felt that they were left to bear the whole burden themselves and that nobody really cared

The desolate scene from Hill 62 and in the town of Ypres.

what became of them. This may have been an unfair view. I am not the person to pass judgement as my views in the matter are definitely prejudiced. But, fair or unfair, it existed and the troops cannot be blamed for holding it. The staff brought it on themselves.

I, myself, was once offered a staff job (at Divisional HQ) but turned it down, against the advice of my CO, to some extent because of this feeling. The CO who pressed me to take it was a regular officer and from a regular's point of view, a job on the staff, even a very junior one, was a good step for a young officer to take if he got the chance. It brought him under the direct notice of the higher authorities and might lead to all sorts of opportunities for extra-regimental advancement. But these arguments did not apply to me. I was only a 'temporary gentleman' and had no intention of staying in the army a day longer than I had to.

The reasons that moved me were different. I shared the common irreverence towards the staff. Not the generals so much; they were considered as just being poor old men, doing as much to help the war effort as their limited mental and physical abilities permitted. But the young and fit men that one saw about as soon as one got well beyond the range of shell fire were looked upon with scorn as gilded popinjays and quite beneath contempt.

In the battalion, I had an established position and some reputation – a cock on a very small dunghill perhaps, but still my own dunghill and I could not give this up to become a gilded popinjay. That sounds like childish vanity, but I think there was more to it than that.

Nobody carried a greater part of the burden of the war than the Poor Bloody Infantry. We knew it and so did the rest of the Army. The term PBI had become almost a title of honour and a member of it could hold his head up in any company anywhere. Also, there was a tremendously strong feeling of loyalty to one's own battalion. The war was undoubtedly bloody, but the men stuck it out in the most appalling conditions without even the slight ameliorations that came the way of a junior officer and you owed it to them and to yourself to stick it out too. They had no illusions left about the war. It was an honour to be accepted by them as an equal and their respect, once earned, was not something to be lightly thrown away for the sake of dry feet and a warm bed.

But I digress. It has already been explained that Passchendaele Ridge was the last of the semi-circle of low hills that encircled Ypres. It rose fairly steeply from our side and, when you looked up at it from the valley below, it was impossible to understand how the Canadians had managed to take it. The valley itself was a morass, due to the small drainage stream at the bottom having been blocked by shell fire and all along the top of the ridge was a line of concrete pill-boxes that completely commanded the slope. It did not seem possible that troops could have struggled through the mud and up the ridge in the face of machine-gun fire from the line of pill-boxes. But they did, though the slaughter on both sides was appalling.

Although the Canadians had taken the ridge and got far enough forward beyond the line of pill-boxes to prevent the Boche from looking down on our side of it, they had not got far enough to enable us to look down on the other side. We were now supposed to advance a few hundred yards to the eastern edge of the ridge, which would give us observation over a large stretch of low-lying country beyond it. The situation was complicated by the fact that the line – that is a manner of speaking only; there was no proper line – ran north-north-west from the north end of Passchendaele village to a place called Teal Cottage. There it bent almost at right-angles and ran due east and west. The result was that the troops on the right were to advance east-north-east while the troops on the left were to advance roughly north. The attack was to be on the night of 1st/2nd December on a two divisional front, the 8th Division – represented by the 25th Brigade – being on the right, from Passchendaele village to Teal Cottage and the 32nd Division on the left. Teal Cottage was a fortified strongpoint at the junction of the two divisions.

The general plan of all our attacks during the time of trench warfare was that a heavy barrage was put down on the enemy's front line to make him keep his head down while we were crossing No Man's Land. The attacking troops were always required to keep as close to their own barrage as possible, even at the risk of incurring casualties from it, so as to be in the enemy's front line before they had time to get up and man their machine-guns after the barrage had passed them. When the barrage lifted, troops went on again close behind it to the second line and so on. Any Boche left behind and not killed or captured in the first attack, were dealt with by 'mopping up parties' detailed for this job, while the front lines of attacking troops moved on.

For this show, the staff put their great brains to work and decided on a surprise attack. It was to start at the unusual hour of 1.55 a.m., instead of just before dawn, and the troops were to dash forward and 'overrun' the enemy's outposts before he knew what was happening. Then our barrage was to come down at zero plus 8 minutes and pulverise the enemy's main position.

This may have looked all right on paper back at GHQ but in fact it was sheer raving lunacy under the existing conditions. To begin with, on the night of 1st/2nd Dec: the moon would be only just past full; there was no cover of any sort, not even a blade of grass, to hide the advance from the enemy; and there was no possibility of rushing forward and 'overrunning' anything; it was only with difficulty that one could advance at all at a dead slow stumble.

All these objections were put forward, to my certain knowledge, by battalion commanders to Brigade and by Brigade to Division. And our Divisional Commander is reported to have backed them up to the Higher Command, saying specifically that 'hostile machine-gun fire from prepared positions on a bright moonlight night was more to be feared than any barrage' and making several alternative suggestions. But he was over-ruled and, in the event, everything went exactly as anticipated; as anticipated, that is, by us and not by the staff.

But that was in the future. First the troops had to be moved up to their jumping-off positions and everything went wrong from the start. To begin with, morale was low. Everybody realised that the whole thing was going to be a shambles. That is not a good mood in which to start any operation. Then, in my opinion, the Boche knew all about it from the start. I feel sure he spotted the REs laying out the jumping-off tapes on the night before the show. Even if I am wrong on this, he had many other chances to learn all about it. There can seldom have been a 'surprise' attack of which so much clear notice was given to the enemy.

There was only one metalled road and one duckboard track available for moving up the troops of the two divisions; the 32nd Division used the road and the 8th Division, i.e. the 25th Brigade, the duckboard track. This track led up to the right of our position and the attacking troops had then to move across the front from right to left, just inside our outpost line. Our battalion was on the extreme left; the moon shone magnificently and it was bright and cold and still. If the Boche did not perceive three battalions straggling right across his front in the bright moonlight, he must have been blind and deaf. It could not have been made more obvious, if we had handed him a written plan of the show on a silver platter.

Also, of course, he knew exactly where all the roads and tracks ran and had registered his guns on them long before. The result was heavy shelling and many casualties on the way up. One company of the Lincolns was reported to have arrived at its jumping off position twenty strong.

I was detailed to be Liaison Officer with the 32nd Division on our left, so I went up the metalled road with them. We also, had a sticky time and one incident must have given the Boche fair warning of what was happening, even if he hadn't known before. As we came up to the top of the ridge, a man carrying a sandbag full of Verey lights and SOS signals was hit by a machine-gun bullet, which set off the flares that he was carrying. He blazed like a torch and though we rolled him in the mud, we couldn't stop the firework display, which must have been visible for miles.

I have mentioned that the junction of the two attacking divisions was at a strong point called Teal Cottage, where the existing line took a right-angled turn. This was supposed to have been captured by the 32nd Division two days previously and it had been so reported. But when we got there we were met with machine-gun fire and found that the Boche were still in possession. This fairly put the cat among the pigeons, because this position was the hinge between the two attacks and could enfilade either one of them. I went off at once to our own Battalion HQ to report this bad news, only to find that they had some more of their own. Roger Brand, our CO, had been wounded and Anderson, the Adjutant, had just got back to HQ after seeing him carried off.

Normally, when the CO becomes a casualty, the next senior officer of the battalion takes charge. But in this show, because of the difficulty of getting hold of any officer from the companies, it had been specifically laid down that the chain of command would go down the people normally at Battalion HQ i.e. first to Anderson, then to me and then to the Regimental Sergeant Major.

We were still pondering on the news about Teal Cottage when the Brigade Major came in and gave us his advice. I was struck by the way he kept on insisting that it was only advice that he was giving. Although Anderson was only a lieutenant and the Brigade Major was, besides being a major, also, in effect, the GSOI of the brigade and the direct representative of the Brigadier, he kept on saying, 'Now, I am not giving you orders. You are in command of the battalion. I am only saying that, if I were in your position, I would try and echelon your left companies back behind Teal Cottage etc. etc., but this is not an order.' But, of course, Anderson was very glad of his advice and immediately went out to try and put it into effect, while the Brigade Major went back to Brigade HQ to report what had happened.

For myself, I sat on in the pill-box and prayed that Anderson would not be hit, because I definitely did not want to take over command of the battalion in these circumstances.

The pill-box was about the size of a smallish kitchen, though of course with a very much lower ceiling; you couldn't stand upright in it. This small space had to contain two Battalion HQ (2nd RB and 2nd Lincolns) and later a third, as the CO of the Irish Rifles, which was in reserve, came forward from his reserve position and remained with us. Only the officers of the three Battalion HQ and some signallers could be accommodated inside the pill-box and even then it was very congested. The rest of the personnel had to find what cover they could in the trench outside. The runners of the Royal Irish Rifles, who always were an undisciplined mob, got at the rum ration and made themselves uproariously drunk and quite useless. When their CO wanted to send messages to his companies, he had to borrow runners from us.

Anderson came back just before zero hour, having done what he could to adjust our line, which wasn't very much, and then we sat, looking at our watches and waiting. Promptly at 1.55 a.m. we heard the Boche machine-guns open up and knew that the attack had started.

And within a very few minutes after that we knew that it had failed. When our barrage came down at zero plus 8, it was a magnificent one – I think the most tremendous I have ever heard. But long before that, the show was over. The Boche machine-guns had eight minutes in which to play unhindered on our troops advancing in bright moonlight and had simply wiped them out. We had advanced about one hundred yards and lost ten officers out of twelve in those few minutes and there was nothing to be done but pick up the pieces.

After the noise had died down, we went out to find out what we could. Men had grouped themselves in shell holes to get what shelter they could, but there was no organisation left and all we could do was to get the groups in touch with each other and pull some back and push others forward to make some sort of coherent line and evacuate as many wounded as we could find. Even this activity had to stop when dawn came, as one could not move about in daylight up at the front.

Back at Battalion HQ however, we were out of sight of the enemy and about eight o'clock I was sent out to look for some more accommodation to relieve the congestion in and around our pill-box. I found another pill-box about two hundred yards down the road but it was choked with dead Germans. They must have been caught by the Canadians and bombed as they were trying to escape. We had to pull out more than a dozen corpses before we could get into it. However, when we got it cleared, it gave us room to sit down and have breakfast and, as there was nothing anyone could do outside, we passed the day in comparative peace.

Only comparative though – there was shelling going on all the time and the Boche seemed to have got our pill-box taped. One shell hit the back wall of the pill-box and burst along the trench outside, causing several casualties. One man caught most of the blast and had one side of his body ripped to pieces. While the stretcher-bearers were trying to bandage him up, he was screaming and groaning, but not because of his terrible wounds. He had got a splinter in the foot away from the side that had been blasted and it appeared to have broken his toe and it was this that he was groaning about. I suppose the side of his body that had been torn to bits was so numb that he did not realise what had happened. But it sounded odd to hear him crying, 'Oh, my toe, oh, my toe' when that was such a minor part of his injuries. Luckily we were able to evacuate him without having to wait for nightfall, but I don't think he can have survived.

We were relieved on the night of 2nd/3rd December and went back to the Wizernes area, just south of St Omer, where we stayed for about three weeks. I wish I knew what our casualties were in this show. I have no figures, but the battalion looked more like a weak company than a proper battalion and everybody felt extremely low.

During this rest period, I was sent down to Boulogne for a couple of days, ostensibly to see about the battalion's Christmas cards, but really, I now believe, to give me a rest and change of scene. Anyway, it was very pleasant to stay in a hotel and wallow in hot baths and sleep in a real bed with sheets.

I had an introduction to a friend's sister, whom I admired greatly and, through her, got to see one of our officers, Cruickshank, who was a friend of mine and who was being nursed in the hospital where she worked. He had been wounded in the Passchendaele show, in the hip, and had had his leg amputated, which had upset him, as he was a great Rugger player and had hoped to play for South Africa.

He told me that, after he was hit, he lay for five hours half in and half out of a shell hole full of stinking water and decaying corpses and when he was found, was sent down to the aid post on the shoulders of four Boche prisoners. He was damned near dead from exhaustion and loss of blood and he said that five times he was dropped from their shoulders when shells came near. You cannot blame the Boche for this; it is extraordinarily difficult not to go flat when you hear a shell coming apparently straight for you; it is a natural and almost involuntary re-action. But think of the agony of being dropped from shoulder height with a broken thigh.

One incident during this rest was an inspection by our corps commander, General Sir Aylmer Hunter-Weston, commonly known as 'Hunter Bunter'. After the formal inspection and while the troops were being closed up for him to address them, he called the officers out and showed them his personal Christmas card, of which he was very proud. He was dancing about on the steps of a house like an excited child, showing us the card and saying, 'There you are, you see. There is the Cloth Hall at Ypres and there is your Corps Commander on his white horse'.

I could not share his enthusiasm. I remember thinking, 'This is the man who controls our lives. We have to go back to Passchendaele and this old fool can do nothing but prattle about his blasted white horse.' I can see now that this was not fair and that I was not normal myself. But it is another example of the gulf between the PBI and the people behind the line.

On Christmas Day, we set out for Passchendaele again, in traditional Christmas weather, with snow and frost, but with no traditional Christmas spirit in our hearts. The very name, Passchendaele, seemed like a lump of lead in your stomach every time you heard it.

We were in and out of the line, never getting back behind Ypres, for the next three weeks. I cannot remember much of the detail. I just retain a general impression of cold and wet and acute exhaustion. It rained and it snowed and it blew; duckboard tracks were washed away; men sank in the mud and were dug out or were drowned or died of exhaustion and exposure. We were alleged to have lost sixty per cent of our strength in one period of three days, without doing any fighting against the Boche. The weather was the worst enemy and nothing mattered but one's desperate effort to survive.

The only morbidly cheerful note was struck by the news that Divisional HQ, in the bank of the Yser Canal, behind Ypres, had been flooded out. It did us good to know that even the staff had had to get their feet wet.

We were finally relieved on 19th January and I remember our final journey out of the line. The relief took all night and we were only just out of sight of the front line when dawn came. Battalion HQ was, of course, the last out, as we could not leave until all the company reliefs had been reported complete. The five miles or so down took hours, partly because of the condition of the ground and partly because we were all so exhausted.

By this time, the RE had managed to get the railway up to Wieltje and we were pleased when we got there, to find a train waiting to take us down to camp behind Vlamertinge. Hot soup had been laid on at Wieltje and that just about saved our lives, as we had had nothing hot inside us for three days. But while this was being dished out, the engine-driver got very excited about the delay. There was some justification for this as the engine was pouring out thick smoke and we were still within range of the larger guns, but we were in no mood to worry about the feelings of an engine-driver who had probably never been nearer the line than he was then.

But when he started blustering and said he would take the train away at once, whether the troops were in it or not, our CO turned to him and threatened to put him up against his own engine and shoot him, if he didn't shut up. He said this so fiercely that the poor engine-driver just wilted and there was not another peep out of him. He probably felt he was being very harshly treated, but these things are comparative, and our men had a thousand times harsher things to put up with.

The train was an English passenger train, with compartments, not horse trucks, and all the doors had been taken off and all the glass taken out of the windows. There was snow on the ground and it was bitterly cold, but in spite of all this, when we finally pulled up at our destination, an hour or so later, not a single man got out. Everyone, from the CO downwards, was dead to the world and the Padre, who had come to meet us with the billeting parties, had to go along the train, shouting and shaking people to wake them up.

We stumbled into camp like a lot of zombies and then we had to stay with the men and force them to eat or they fell asleep over their mess-tins. After we had tucked them up, we rolled up in our own blankets and the whole camp slept for about eighteen hours.

That was the last I saw of Passchendaele and I was never so glad to get out of a place in my life. We had other sticky times, but nothing in the whole war was anything like the Ypres front and, in particular, the Passchendaele sector of it.

IX

Instructor in Blighty

About this time a change was made in the organisation of the division and the number of battalions in each brigade was reduced from four to three. This was supposed to have been made necessary by the shortage of man-power caused by the heavy casualties, but I could not understand the arithmetic of it. It seemed to me, and still does, that if you have 12 divisions of 3 brigades with 4 battalions in each, you have 144 battalions. And if you change this into 16 divisions of 3 brigades with 3 battalions in each, you may have more divisions, but you still have only 144 battalions. The only difference that I can see is that, to put the same number of men in the line you have to find staff for 4 extra divisional headquarters, and I fail to understand how this can relieve a man-power shortage. But I am afraid I have not got the proper staff brain power.

Anyway, we lost the 2nd Lincolns and the 2nd Royal Irish Rifles and gained the 2nd East Lancs. The 2nd Lincolns and the 2nd East Lancs were good battalions and the exchange was a fair one. The Royal Irish Rifles were the sort of people who never did any wiring or revetting in their part of the line and who dug cubby-holes under the parapet, thus weakening the trench, and to take over a stretch of line from them always meant more work for the incoming battalion. Their departure was no great loss. But, to be fair to the Irish, it must be said that most of their men appeared to come from Whitechapel or thereabouts, and were not truly representative of the 'Ould Country'.

About this time too, a scheme was produced for giving officers who had been in the line a long time, a spell at home. I am not sure whether the offer was for a month's leave or three months' duty at home or both. Anyway, volunteers were asked for. It sounded too good to be true and either because of this or because people were reluctant to leave their battalions, volunteers were not forthcoming. So battalions were instructed to detail people and I was detailed by my battalion. I did not know exactly what I was detailed for, but I was instructed to go home, report myself to the War Office by letter and await instructions.

I cannot pretend that I was sorry, but I do not think that I expected to be away as long as I was, because, after I had been at home at Cheltenham for a couple of weeks, I remember thinking that I must have been forgotten and would soon be arrested as a deserter, so I wrote another letter to the War Office to remind them that I was still at home, awaiting orders. The idea behind this was that it would show, if the MP came after me, that I was not deliberately hiding.

In the event, I had a full month at home before my orders came through. I cannot remember anything in particular about this leave. Probably I slept a good deal of the time, for I was very tired.

When my orders did come through, they were to join the Suffolk Yeomanry at Woodbridge, in Suffolk. In peace-time, the Suffolk Yeomanry were a territorial cavalry unit, but now their horses had been withdrawn and they were mounted on bicycles. So I was in the odd position of being a Rifleman teaching line drill to a cavalry unit mounted on bicycles. The battalion consisted almost entirely of young soldiers who had been weeded out from all sorts of different regiments as being too young to go to France. The CO, the Adjutant and the Quartermaster were elderly men who had not been to France and the rest of the officers were people like myself, who had been a long time in the line or had been too badly wounded to be able to return to the front.

The two elements did not mix very well. The older men seemed to resent the influx of a horde of youngsters and I daresay we were cocky and intolerant. But though we were young, we had all had a lot of front line experience and we did know something about the war as it was actually being fought. And one result of our experience was that we did appreciate how important was the relationship between officers and men.

This had been forcibly impressed on me very early in my career. Soon after I joined the RB, a case had occurred when, after a long march, an officer had seen his men into billets, inspected their feet and so on, but had not actually waited to see them fed. When the food came up, it was bad. The platoon sergeant coped with the situation and got some bully beef or something as a substitute, but the officer got in the hell of a row because he had not been there to see to it himself.

Moreover, the CO called the rest of the junior officers together and gave us a very severe lecture. He said that a subaltern, in his own right, was a very low form of life. His only reason for existing at all was to look after his men. He was entirely responsible for his platoon's health, welfare, training and efficiency. The NCOs were there to help him do this, but not to do the job for him and he could not pass his responsibilities on to them. We had batmen to look after us, not because we were privileged people, but solely to enable us to give more of ourselves to our jobs and if he found an officer putting his own comfort before that of his men, he would break him mercilessly, whatever the circumstances.

Roger Brand was a first-class CO and not just a martinet. He followed his own ruling himself and insisted that everybody else did too and I am sure that it was because of this that the 2nd RB was such a good battalion. And the men knew it too. We might feel forlorn and forsaken in places like Passchendaele, but at least the men knew that their own officers were in the mud with them up to their necks and doing what they could, even though that wasn't much.

And it paid dividends. I shall tell, later, of incidents when men who did not know me personally, stood by me in sticky situations simply because we wore the same cap-badge and expected to be able to rely on each other.

With this background, we were quite shocked at the methods in use in our new battalion. The Adjutant laid down in orders the details of the training programme to be followed each day and when we had been allotted to our various companies and platoons, we naturally took charge and started to carry out the training programme. The sergeant instructors protested and said the training was their job. We said we thought it was ours. The CO, when appealed to, supported the instructors and, in effect, told us to run away and play and leave the men to the sergeant-instructors.

The author on leave at Cheltenham. 'Probably I slept a good deal of the time, for I was very tired.'

This decision appalled us. There is so much more to training than just teaching men to form fours or aim a rifle. You cannot form an efficient unit, or even a unit of any sort, by just saying, 'Carry on, sergeant' and walking away. It is absolutely essential to work with the men all day and every day and get to know them as individuals.

Moreover, some of the sergeant-instructors were not very good types. One or two were loud-mouthed braggarts who thought they were little tin gods, because nobody had ever dared to stand up to them. But we newcomers had no use for fit men, however big and blustery, who got a pain in their big toes whenever a draft was in the offing. We all knew men who had been wounded and patched up and sent back to the front, many more than once, and it was an offence to us that healthy men should still be sitting at home in 1918, when better men than they were being sent back to the slaughter again and again.

So we had no sympathy with the draft-dodgers. They soon found out that we were tougher than they were and their bluff and bluster evaporated till they were deflated to their normal size.

I was less troubled by this sort of thing than some. Because I had had my flags up in the Artists, I was put in charge of the Signal Section, and as this was a specialist's job, I was more or less left alone. Also my Signal Sergeant was not a bully or a blusterer, but just a bit thick in the head. He knew something about the technical side of the work but had no idea how to train men. I found the section pretty bad at morse and fed up with practising it, which they dodged whenever they could. Of course, after you have learned the letters, speed in morse is almost entirely a question of practice. And practising the same thing over and over again is bound to be dull unless you can feel that it is doing you some good and that you are making progress.

They could send fairly fast but rather badly and when the chap at the other end failed to get the message, they tended to curse him for a dolt. The first rule I made was that, when a message was not correctly received, it would be considered that the sender was at fault and he would have to send it again and again at slower and slower speeds until it was received correctly.

This was an entirely new point of view and at first they thought

I was mad. But as the sender had to go on repeating the message till it was correctly received, he eventually found that it was worth while taking the trouble to send it both slowly and accurately. And when he did that, the receiver would find that he was not such a dolt as he had been led to believe and that he really could read morse when it was properly sent. Once the importance of accurate sending had been established in everybody's minds, we could start working up speeds and soon the men were getting really keen and boasting to each other about their skills. And, of course, getting rid of the atmosphere of lethargy and boredom brought an all-round improvement and it was not long before we were sticking out our chests and thinking we were the most important unit in the battalion.

Apart from training, our duties included the defence of the East Coast against invasion. The defence scheme was a curious mixture of careful planning on the one hand and either ignorance or idiocy on the other. Our battle position was on the beach near Alderton, just north of Bawdsey and we had to proceed there on receipt of a code-word by telephone. The Orderly Officer had to sleep in the Orderly Room, so that there was always someone there to receive the message and, on receipt of the code-word, he had to turn the battalion out.

We never knew whether the code-word indicated the real thing or just a practice. When we were ready to move off, we had to report to Brigade and sometimes the practice was cancelled at this point. At other times we had to ride out to Alderton, about eight miles away and man our position until such time as we were told to come home again.

The turn-out was pretty slack. Machine-guns and ammunition were carried on platforms fixed between two bicycles. On one occasion, the machine-gun officer found that, though the ammunition boxes were in place on their platforms, they were quite empty. He raised Cain and the troops were quite aggrieved. Machine-gun ammunition was heavy stuff and what was the use of lugging it all the way out to the coast and back again, when everybody knew there was not going to be an invasion? That was the sort of attitude that prevailed.

There was a certain amount of plausibility about this argument, because an invasion was not likely at that stage of the war, but a raid in force was still a distinct possibility and, anyway, it was not an attitude that could be allowed. Everybody always thinks, 'It can't happen here', but in war it can – and does. It was quite sound and reasonable to have a defence scheme and to practise it frequently and properly.

The less sensible part of the defence planning came to light when we got to our battle position. The coast at Alderton is low-lying, with two or three miles of marsh-land behind it. This is intersected by dykes and would be difficult to traverse unless you knew the paths and where the dykes could be crossed. To my mind, the obvious defence position was on the first rising ground behind the marshes. Machine-guns and light artillery up there could have commanded the whole area and made things extremely difficult for a landing force straggling across the marshes to get to grips with them.

But our positions were on the beach itself. The trenches were dug in the shingle and revetted with sand-bags of shingle. Presumably we were there to fire at an invading force while it was coming to shore in small boats. But no one would have tried to put a force on shore in small boats without a covering force and shell fire from that would have made the beach a death trap. High-explosive shells bursting on the beach would have converted the shingle into an unlimited supply of shrapnel and the trenches would have collapsed and buried the occupants if a shell had landed anywhere near them. If a bombardment by the covering force had started when the small boats set out, I doubt if there would have been half-a-dozen men left alive on the beach by the time they got within rifle range.

Another thing was that the coast was dotted with Martello Towers, that stood out from the flat landscape like sore thumbs. They would have been the obvious marks on which a covering force would have ranged its guns. Yet the CO made one of these his Battalion HQ and we had a row about this.

I refused to put my Signal Section into the Martello Tower. The CO said he wanted his signallers with him. I said that I was responsible for the communications of the battalion and that it was a technical job that I should be allowed to do in my own way.

I proposed to set up the Signal Station on the edge of the marsh behind the beach and about two hundred yards to one side of the Martello Tower and run all my wires to this point. I would keep up communication between Battalion HQ and the Signal Station by means of runners. I just managed to refrain from telling him that there would not be any Martello Tower or Battalion HQ after the first ten minutes of a real show.

He wouldn't see it, but I finally got my way by saying that I would do what he wanted only if he gave me a direct order to do so and took responsibility for it. I would then report the matter to the Brigade Signal Officer and give my reasons for thinking that the Battalion communication system was unsatisfactory.

I realise now that we must have been an awful nuisance to the unfortunate CO. All he wanted was a quiet life, but the Higher Command appeared to be taking the defence system seriously and I felt that, if we were going to take part in it at all, we should do so realistically.

Apart from disagreements with elderly senior officers and the stirring up of draft dodgers who thought they had dug themselves into a cushy job for the duration, we had a good time at Woodbridge. I had a very good billet in the house of a rich, old bachelor, who was looked after by a nice old married couple, the husband acting as butler and the wife as housekeeper and cook. I was the only man billeted there and they were all very kind to me.

I was made free of the library, which was a large room lined with books from floor to ceiling and with French windows that opened on to a well-kept lawn and grass paths lined with daffodils. I had to eat in the mess, but otherwise I spent most of my spare time in my billet and was treated like a son of the house. I would find my slacks neatly laid out for me in the evenings and one night when there was an invasion scare and we were turned out just before midnight, the old lady insisted on getting up to make me sandwiches, while her husband and my host also got up and fussed over me with the greatest concern. I was thoroughly spoilt and petted and I regret that I never showed my gratitude and appreciation adequately.

We did not, however, have to defend the East Coast for very long, because the brigade, of which we formed part, was transferred to Ireland. We went an all-night journey by train to Holyhead via York, though that seems a roundabout way to get to Holyhead from Suffolk.

When we got to Holyhead, we were treated to another brilliant piece of staff work. All the troops were put into one ship and all the equipment into another. On arrival at Kingstown – they call it something else now, but I mean the port of Dublin – the troops were marched to camp and the equipment, when it arrived, was unloaded and spread out all along the quay. Then each of the battalions sent down a party to grab its own share. None of the stuff was marked in any way, so it was a case of first come, first served. We got to work early and my share of the loot was a new motor bike. The late-comers had to put up with the broken bits and pieces.

I should explain that, because we were a cyclist battalion, we had no horses or horse transport. The CO and Adjutant had a car and the other officers who would normally have been mounted, were provided with motor bikes, and my position as Signal Officer entitled me to one of these. They were light-weight Triumphs that had been withdrawn from France as it was found that they could not stand up to the French cobbles.

We went first to a camp in the Curragh and then, after a day or two, out to the north-west of the country. Brigade Headquarters was at Carrick-on-Shannon and half our battalion was at Sligo and the other half at Boyle, a little town in the extreme North West of County Roscommon.

I was at Boyle. It was in lovely country and we were quartered in a barracks just off the main square.

A river ran along one side of the barrack square and the troops used to sit on the wall and fish for salmon with bent pins.

The 1916 rebellion had long been put down but the country was still a bit disturbed. The local gentry were very glad to see us and did all they could to make us welcome. But when you went to dinner at one of the big country houses, your host usually opened the front door on the chain and with a revolver in his hand. This was after dark though; during the day we were given ghillies to try fly-fishing in what were, normally, strictly preserved waters, but which had not now been fished for several years. We never caught anything, but it was fun trying.

The rest of the population were not over-friendly, though there was not much overt hostility. Our despatch riders used to go about in pairs and sometimes got a brick chucked at them, but the only evidence of antagonism that I, personally, observed was an occasional child popping up from behind a stone wall and shouting 'Up the rebels'.

We had very little to do with the ordinary people so their attitude did not bother us, but what I did not like about them was their two-facedness. If there were six English soldiers in a pub and two Irishmen, the Irishmen were all over the troops, standing them drinks and turning on the blarney at full pressure. But if there were six Irishmen and only two soldiers, the chances were that the troops would come home with bloody noses and broken heads.

But it takes the Irish to manage the Irish and I was interested to see how it was done. It happened that two of the 1916 rebels were let out of gaol while we were there. A reception for them was organised in Boyle and it was thought that there might be trouble. The RIC asked that the troops should be kept in barracks, ready for use if need be, but that we should not interfere unless they asked for our help.

The reception committee, with some hundreds of citizens and two bands, marched down to the station to receive the heroes and then came back and held a meeting in the town square. The local big-wigs climbed on carts and addressed the multitude. Then the heroes had their say and then more people started speechifying, till there must have been half a dozen people on carts, talking, and a couple of thousand altogether in the square.

I was Orderly Officer and was watching all this from a window in the barracks that overlooked the square. Things were beginning to warm up nicely, when one constable of the RIC appeared at one corner of the square. He didn't do anything; just stood there. Then another policeman appeared and stood at another corner and people started looking furtively over their shoulders. Then yet one more policeman came and stood at a third corner and more and more people seemed to be getting apprehensive and started slipping away in ones and twos.

To cut a long story short, within ten minutes there were only the speakers and a couple of dozen spectators left and when these were told to go home, they meekly did so.

I was very impressed by this. If troops had been used to line the square in an attempt to overawe the populace and keep order by force, it was quite likely that a nasty riot might have developed. But the RIC dispersed the whole crowd with only three men visible (though I dare say there were others in reserve) and without any bloodshed and yet enabled them to let off a lot of hot air and see themselves as bold defiant rebels. It was a triumph of mind over matter.

It appeared that there had not been any British troops in this part of Ireland for a long time. While the landowners welcomed us, some of the others, with guilty consciences, were apprehensive and the wildest rumours to account for our presence were circulated. The official view, however, was that our being there was a guarantee that law and order would prevail and all those people who had guns of their own, whether for self-defence or for less reputable reasons, were ordered to hand them in. We collected a large variety of all sorts of fire-arms, but I have no doubt that many more continued to be clandestinely held.

Several years after the war was over, I got a letter from the War Office, stating that on such and such a date I had signed a receipt for such and such weapons from Mr So and So and what had I done with them? Of course, I didn't know what had become of them. When they were handed in, we put them in our guard-room and they were eventually taken away to Brigade. What happened to them after that was not our business. I hope the old chap got his guns back but I should not think it very likely.

The meticulousness of the War Office over petty accounting details caused a certain amount of rueful amusement. For instance, in France we drew a field allowance of 2/6 a day. This, more or less, corresponded to the Navy's 'hard-lying' pay and was supposed to compensate us for using our own camp equipment when the Army could not provide proper quarters. When we came home, this was withdrawn. That was fair enough when we were in comfortable billets, as we were at Woodbridge. But it was also withdrawn while we were in Ireland, on the plea that we were occupying furnished quarters in barracks. But the quarters consisted of one room in which six officers had to sleep and the furniture was one wooden washstand containing a china jug and basin.

On another occasion, I overpaid a man who was going on leave. You were not supposed to pay a man more than the balance due to him as shown by his pay-book. This man's book shewed that he had five francs due. The official rate of exchange was 25 francs to the pound, so five francs was about 4/– (20p). You couldn't send a man on leave with five francs. His leave was, to the individual, the most important thing in the whole war. It came round seldom enough in all conscience and anything that interfered with leave was more important than the loss of any battle. So I paid this man 25 or 50 francs and did it with a clear conscience. But the overpayment was charged up to my account until he had worked it off and, if he had been killed before that happened, I should have had to bear it. I would not have minded, but it did strike me as being pretty pettifogging.

However, this is by the way. While we were luxuriating in Ireland, things had not been going well in France. The Boche had brought troops over from the Russian front and mounted two big attacks, one on the Somme front and one just south of Ypres. In both cases, he had advanced a long way before being held up and casualties had been very heavy, so we were not surprised when telegrams began coming in recalling us to France. Reinforcements that could and should have been sent out before the Boche struck were now being rushed to France, but the Suffolk Yeomanry were nearly all young, under-age soldiers, so we did not go out as a unit and the long service men, like myself, were recalled, as individuals, to our own battalions.

I was very glad of that. Not that I wanted to go back, but if I had to, I very much preferred to go back to the RB. I should not have enjoyed going into action with people who knew so little about warfare as the Suffolk Yeomanry, in spite of their staff of sergeant instructors.

X

Back to the Line

When I got back to France, I found that the 8th Division had moved down to the Champagne country and were in the line near Berry-au-Bac, about ten miles north-north-west of Rheims. This was in the French part of the line and four of the British divisions that had been most severely cut up in the previous retreats had been sent down there for a 'rest'. God knows why, because it was common knowledge, among army and civilians alike, that the Boche was preparing his next attack on this front. It was in no sense a secret, not even an 'open' one and the only point in doubt was the exact date on which it would start.

Anyway, this meant that we had to go through Paris and as a fellow I was travelling with wanted to look up some friends, we decided to take twenty-four hours there. We seemed to spend most of the time in the Metro, but finally this chap found his friends and we had dinner with them.

The next day we got as far as Fere-en-Tardenois. I remember the name because, two or three days later, a battalion that was being rushed up by rail, suddenly found themselves under fire there and had to get out and fight a little battle though, until it started, they had no idea that they were anywhere near the enemy.

We had dinner that night with a most amusing young French officer and the next morning went on as far as Fismes. I forget why we were turned out there, because it was still a long way from the front and the show had not yet started. I was mooning about in Fismes, trying to find some way of getting myself and my kit up to Berry-au-Bac, when I came across our own mess-cart, which had come down to get supplies of some sort. That solved my problem and, by the afternoon, I was in our transport lines.

These were in a wood – a real wood with big trees still standing and in full leaf, not the collection of splintered trunks that passed for a wood in the Ypres sector. I reported my arrival and was told that, as the battalion was due to come out of the line the next night, it was not worth while my coming up for just one day, so I was to remain at the transport lines and take charge of 'details'. This means all the odd bodies – men coming from or going on leave or courses, slightly sick men and so on.

The line we were holding in this sector was from one to two miles deep on the north bank of the Aisne. The obvious thing to do, once we knew that an attack was coming, would have been to withdraw all troops but a few out-posts to the south of the river and blow up the bridges, leaving the Boche with the difficult task of crossing the Aisne under heavy fire from the heights on our side. According to my history book, this was strongly urged by the British divisional generals when they took over the line. But the French, who were in command in this area, refused to allow an inch of the sacred soil of France to be given up. So all our forward troops and most of our guns were on the wrong side of the river when the attack started.

The result was what had been expected by everyone except the staff and by eight o'clock the next morning our divisional artillery had exactly one gun left.

However, I knew nothing of all this at the time. I went to sleep comfortably in a hut in the transport lines until about four in the morning, (27th May) when I was woken up by gas shells falling in the camp. I had a moment of panic when I couldn't find my gas mask. It was quite close; I just couldn't lay my hands on it immediately in the dark. (Oddly enough this was the only one of my war experiences that kept coming back to me in the form of a nightmare for a number of years after the war was over.)

As soon as I had found my mask, I went over to the men's hut. They were sitting up and arguing as to whether it was necessary to put their masks on. The concentration of gas was getting quite heavy by this time, so I told them to put on their masks and get dressed and then stand-by for further orders.

Soon rumours began to circulate of disaster at the front, but we did not then know the extent of it and it was full daylight before we got orders to move back to some place, whose name I forget, but which was a good distance to the rear.

There was only one road exit from the wood we were in. It was a dirt track that curved down from the back of the wood to join a main road in the valley below. The Boche had it taped and were dropping five-nines on it at about one every minute or a little less. Our battalion transport were lined up just inside the wood and as soon as a shell had exploded the GS wagon or limber at the head of the line would dash out at full gallop to try and get past the danger point before the next shell arrived.

We, the 'details', since we had no horses to worry about, did not have to run the gauntlet, but got out of the wood by climbing through the fence that surrounded it at some distance from the road exit. But we stopped for a little to watch the transport getting out. It was very exciting, something like a Roman chariot race, with the horses made frantic by the explosions and the drivers lashing them through the smoke of one shell to get clear before the next.

We marched back with the transport to the village to which they had been told to go and there we began to learn from stragglers something of what had happened at the front. The HQ of the 25th Brigade had been surrounded before they even knew that the front line had gone. Pascoe, who had had to cope with our inefficiencies when we had first joined the RB had been promoted and was at this time acting as the brigade major of the 25th Brigade and he had led the HQ staff out to do battle when they found themselves surrounded. As would have been expected by any one who knew him, he had put up a very good show, but had been killed. My informant had been captured at the same time. He had been disarmed and then left with one sentry while the rest of the Boche went on. He had escaped by taking off his tin hat and suddenly crashing the sharp edge of it into the sentry's face and making a bolt for it. That seemed to me pretty clever. I don't think I would have thought of using a tin hat as a weapon.

About ten o'clock that night, I was sent up the line with a motley party of about fifty men, cooks, batmen, clerks and so on from all sorts of regiments. A major put us in an old quarry on the top of a hill, with the lip of the quarry facing the enemy.

We posted sentries, but nothing happened all night and we got some rest. Shortly before dawn, we stood-to along the top edge of the quarry and as it got light we could see that it was very misty. Then figures started appearing out of the mist and we opened fire, but it was rather ineffective, because you could only see one or two men at a time and they loomed up out of the mist and were lost in it again before you could get a good shot at them. Then someone away on the left started shouting that we were being surrounded and the cry was taken up and everyone rushed away. I was glad there was no one in authority to see it or I should have been blamed, though there wasn't really much I could do.

In theory, I suppose I should have shot one or two men, though that wouldn't have stopped any but perhaps half a dozen men close to me, if that. But it's pretty silly shooting your own men, I think, and in any event, that course of action did not occur to me at the time.

Within a few seconds, the only people left in the quarry were myself and my batman, who was brewing tea down in the quarry itself. He was the only man from the RB in the party, but he did not know me and I did not know him. I had merely picked him out from the 'details' on the previous night because I had not yet had a batman allotted to me. Yet he stayed when everyone else ran away and the only conceivable reason was that we wore the same cap-badge. That is one instance of what good relations between officers and men in a good battalion can mean.

I said to him, 'Well, we can't hold this place by ourselves, so we had better get out while we can' and we followed the rest down into the valley.

On the other side of the valley, the ground rose sharply in an open grass-covered hill, just like one of our South Downs. There was a cart-track that ran diagonally up it and people were pouring along it. At places, the road had been dug into the hill so that there was a bank of earth on the outer side that afforded cover. Then there would be a gap and then another sheltered stretch and so on. The Boche were playing machine-guns along the track and the sheltered stretches afforded places where one could stop and get one's breath. There would be a little group of men waiting in each and from time to time, a few would make a dash across the open gap to the next piece of shelter. If you waited till a machine-gun had fired a burst, you stood a good chance of getting across and under cover again before the next burst.

I was just dashing across one such gap when the man next to me suddenly whirled round with his hands clapped to his face. I caught him and dragged him into shelter and then saw that he had got a machine-gun bullet through the face. It had gone in at one cheek and out at the other and had not touched his teeth. It was a marvellous escape. If you want to understand how marvellous, try pushing a finger into your cheek and feel how little room there is between your teeth, even with your mouth wide open. If the bullet had hit his teeth it would at least have smashed his jaw even if it had not been deflected into his brain and killed him.

I was just walking over the crest of this hill, when I felt a blow on the back of my neck, which knocked me forward on to my knees. I thought, 'My God, I've been hit', but it didn't hurt and I knew I wasn't dead, so I put my hand up and felt a bullet sticking out of my neck. It must have been just about spent, because it had penetrated the collar of my tunic and my shirt collar, but had only gone a very little way into my neck, so that I could pluck it out with my fingers. Which I did and that was the end of the matter. It never gave me any trouble afterwards.

Over the crest of the hill, out of direct machine-gun fire, we started collecting the men as they came up, with the idea of forming a line and putting up some sort of resistance. The men were not panicking. They were quite willing to stop; they only wanted someone to tell them what to do.

After a little while, I thought I had better find out what was going on on our right, so that we could extend our line that way and cover the whole of the front of the hill. I left another officer with orders to go on collecting stragglers and, taking a corporal with me, went off along the top of the hill towards a wood.

I didn't expect to find anyone really, because I thought that it was only our little part of the line that had given way and that the rest of our troops were probably still on the far side of the valley across which we had come. But we had only gone about a hundred yards into the wood, when we suddenly saw a Boche patrol of six men in front of us, about fifty yards away. They saw us at the same time and we all stood staring at each other with our mouths open.

The Boche recovered first. One of them dropped on his knee and aimed at us. That stirred me into action and I fell backwards down a bank I had just climbed, hauling the corporal after me by his coat collar. Unfortunately, this precipitate action made him let go of his rifle. That left the two of us, with only my revolver between us, against six Boche and it didn't seem to me to be a good idea to stay and fight it out, so we turned and ran – not the way we had come, but straight down-hill through the wood towards the rear. The whole place seemed to be alive with Germans and we ran and dodged behind trees and ran again like enthusiastic Boy Scouts on a Saturday afternoon.

Thinking it over now, I realise that there was no real evidence that there was a single Boche in that wood, other than the patrol we saw at the beginning. But we thought there were and the thought lent wings to our feet and we didn't stop to enquire if the rustlings we heard were really only made by birds and squirrels.

At the bottom of the hill was a big château with a lovely walled orchard. We got into this by a little green door on the side nearest the enemy and then ran all round it like frightened rabbits, looking for a way out on the other side. But we couldn't find one and finally the corporal had to make a back for me so that I could scramble up to the top of the wall. Then, sitting astride it, I leant down and hauled him up.

We went through the stables of the château and found ourselves on a wooden causeway running across a marsh. The Boche had a machine-gun playing on it from somewhere out of sight and it was very funny to watch other stragglers lifting their feet up and dancing like a cat on hot bricks or someone doing the Cake-Walk, whenever the bullets came near. But ridiculous as I knew it to be, I found myself doing exactly the same thing.

At the end of this causeway, we found a captain from another brigade trying to organise a line. I plonked myself down behind a tree and was glad of a breathing spell, but very soon I was told to go off to the left and find out what was happening there.

I intended to go and then come back and report to this captain within a short time, so I left my pack where I had been lying.

That was a mistake, because I never did get back and had to spend some weeks running about France with practically no kit at all – not even a razor.

When I got out of the wood, I found myself in a broad open basin with troops scattered about all over it. A couple of officers were trying to form a line along a road that ran down the middle. I talked to them and learned that they were trying to form a defensive flank and was just thinking about going back to report, when a German field gun battery galloped up to the top of the ridge above the basin, unlimbered and opened fire on us.

Being fired at by guns over open sights was a new experience and a shattering one.

The shells arrived with such a vicious whizz and each one seemed to be aimed at you personally. I was not the only one who found it unnerving. Everyone did and the whole lot of us just broke and ran.

This was the only time I saw a real rout. It is true that we had been retreating the whole day, but not, most of the time, on the run and we had had in mind the finding of a position where we could make a stand. But now it was just panic flight, with each man, including me, thinking of nothing but saving his own skin.

We felt a little safer when we got into a small wood on a hill-side. It wasn't really any better because the shells kept on arriving, but, with cover from view, you could feel that the enemy were not shooting at you personally and that it would just be bad luck if you happened to get hit. Nevertheless, we didn't stop until we were over the top of the hill and out of the way of direct fire.

Then we had a lull as we had temporarily out-distanced the Boche infantry and we used it to reorganise a bit. I found myself on the top of a hill with a valley behind me that rose up to another, higher whale-backed hill, again just like our South Downs. To my right, it was all open country while on the left was a big wood that ran down from our position into the valley and up to the top of the hill behind. I could see British troops on my right, but nothing on my left until two French officers came out of the wood and started lining up their men on my left. They took no notice of us whatever, but made their dispositions as though we were not there. That was rather shame-making, but very sensible of them, because they had no reason to think that we were to be relied on. They were both much older men than me and their actions gave me confidence as they seemed to be quite calm and to know what they were doing. Also, as long as they were there, I knew my left flank was secure.

No Boche appeared on our front, but soon the line on our right began to give way and we could see the enemy beginning to force their way down into the valley.

I swung up my little group back at right angles to form a defensive flank and fired along the valley at the Boche we could see. It was a sound enough idea, but not very effective as we never seemed to hit anybody.

Then the French went back and I deduced that the enemy were pressing forward on our left also. I didn't want to be left all alone out in front of everybody else, so we also withdrew. We went into the wood to get cover from view as we went down across the valley and up the other side. Machine-gun bullets were shattering through the trees, but the Boche couldn't see us once we were twenty or thirty yards inside the wood and we got to the top without damage.

Then we came out of the wood and joined up with the rest of the troops that were already there, stretched out in a long line right along the top of the hill.

They were, quite naturally, standing back from the crest of the hill, where they couldn't be reached by fire from the enemy below. But this meant that they also could not fire on the advancing Boche and it was necessary to advance the line until the men could see over the top and fire down the hill-side.

It only meant going forward ten or twenty yards, but there was considerable reluctance to move that short distance. After all, if you put yourself in a position to fire at the enemy, you also put yourself in a position where he can fire at you and most of the men had had enough of being shot at for the time being.

You had to take small groups of half a dozen men and bring them forward inch by inch. Only those men who were almost within touch would come and they came forward slowly step by step as though they had wooden legs.

Kipling, as usual, has expressed it exactly:

'So, like a man in irons, which isn't glad to go
They moves 'em off by companies, uncommon stiff and slow.'

Kipling was never in action, as far as I know, but that is just how the men moved, 'uncommon stiff and slow'.

Once we had got them forward, we managed to keep the Boche pinned down for quite a long time – the best part of two hours, I should think. Then right along at the far end of the hill, they got a trench mortar into action. It was too far away to affect us, but I remember seeing one shell explode alongside a man on a horse. Both were lifted right off the ground, the man higher than the horse so that you could see daylight between him and the saddle, and they both hung in the air for what seemed minutes until they toppled over.

While the trench mortar fire did not reach us, it must have done a lot of damage on the far right because it enabled the Boche to get a machine-gun up on that flank and it suddenly opened fire right along the crest and the whole line went. This was retreat again, but it wasn't panic flight. If you get enfiladed by machine gun fire from a flank, it is just common-sense to get out of the way. You can't do any good by staying, however brave you are; you just get killed. I did see one man turn back to pick up another who had been wounded. It was superlatively brave and I wouldn't have done it for anything or anybody, but it was quite useless. It just meant two casualties instead of one.

After we had been driven off this hill crest and as we were going back to find another one to sit on, we passed a French battery of .75s manned by Moroccans. We were very pleased to see them, because they were the first signs of artillery support that we had seen all day, but they were not pleased to see us. The little fat French major in command was foaming at the mouth and waving his stick at us and calling us cowards and traitors.

It was interesting to see how the troops took this. They may not have understood the exact words, but his meaning was unmistakable. The troops just looked at him as one would at a child in a temper. 'Poor little chap, he doesn't understand. But he will grow up and find out.'

Unfortunately, the major's skill was apparently not up to his burning patriotism. His battery opened fire soon afterwards and plonked shell after shell into a position held by our troops. We could see the shells landing and the troops scattering. It is bad enough to be shelled over open sights by the enemy. It must be even more demoralising to be shelled in the back by your own batteries.

I cannot remember much about the next few weeks, but it was the most idyllic part of the war. The 8th Division had ceased to exist as a division. There was no organisation and no orders. When you found men straggling about, you attached them to your little group and just wandered about the countryside, sitting on a hill top till you were pushed off it and then wandering back to the next one. The ASC left dumps of rations and ammunition at prominent points like cross-roads and as you wandered by you helped yourself to what you needed.

The weather was lovely and there was very little shelling. At nights, we dug ourselves small trenches and lined them with branches and leaves and lay in them in great comfort. It was rather like lying in a coffin, but there was no hardship in sleeping out in the soft summer nights. We even tried a bit of looting, but a French refugee does not leave much behind him, even when he is fleeing from an invader. All I got of any use was a bottle of plums preserved in alcohol. Oh, and some horse clippers. We used these to clip our hair, so that we looked like a bunch of convicts.

Our little group consisted of three officers and between fifty and seventy men. One of the officers adopted the pose of a very la-di-dah Man about Town and made out that he could not bear to smoke ration cigarettes – nothing but the very best cigars. But before long, he was concocting the most poisonous smokes out of leaves and brown paper, which made him feel sick.

After about three weeks of this delightful existence, the Boche advance ran out of steam, the situation was stabilised and the Army caught up with us. They organised a composite battalion out of all the odds and ends of the 8th Division and we had to go all regimental again. The fighting got stiffer too, but I can only remember one incident, when the Boche used gas shells to saturate a wood we were in. One man had inhaled enough gas, before he put his mask on, to make him vomit and I can remember two of us struggling to hold his mask on his face while he was being sick inside it. Most unpleasant, but he would have died if he had been allowed to take it off.

The end of the retreat, as far as I was concerned, was when we marched into an American hutted camp somewhere near Epernay. The Americans had been in the war for some time, but had seen practically no fighting and this particular camp housed an infantry unit, which had recently arrived in France. They were being sent up to quiet parts of the line in small parties to have a look at the war before they went into the line as a unit.

We must have looked a fine bunch of scarecrows when we marched in. I myself had a month's growth of beard on my face and a cropped head like a convict. We had not had a bath or our clothes off for a month and must have smelt like badgers. But the Americans were very good to us. They bathed us and fed us and gave up their bunks to us. I was too tired to show my appreciation at the time. I just had a bath and fell into a bunk and slept and slept and slept. I have no idea whether it was for 12 hours or 24 or even 36. It might have been any length of time, but as I came back to consciousness, I was aware of a tall figure standing by my bunk, who said, 'Say, Lootenant, d'you want the hair-kid?' This had no meaning whatever to me, but as I opened one bleary eye, he said it again. I struggled out of the depths vainly trying to understand this foreign language and somebody eventually translated. The tall figure was the regimental barber and he wanted to know if I needed his services.

Mention of the barber reminds me of an incident that almost led to a rupture of Allied relations. As I have told already, the little bunch of men that had been with me had had their heads cropped with horse-clippers, but most of the rest had their hair down over their collars in most unmilitary fashion. In addition to their other kindnesses, the Americans cut all the troops' hair and I was deputed to offer them payment at the British Army rate of 2½d a man. I protested because I knew it would cause a row. In the first place, they didn't want to be paid at all. They did it out of pure good-will. And in the second place, the rate of 2½d a man was to them, so ludicrous that it sounded like an insult.

But the major who was in command of the composite battalion got very angry with me. He said he didn't want to be told his business by a lieutenant. I had received an order and I would carry it out immediately or I would be placed under arrest. So there was nothing I could do but obey.

The Americans, as I expected, blew right up, once they had overcome their incredulity and understood what I was offering. But I was grateful that they realised that I was only the messenger boy and did not take their anger out on me. Their CO went off to see our CO and I hope gave him hell, but the matter was no longer in my hands. Still, I thought then, and still do, that it was a pretty oafish thing to do.

I have nothing but praise for the way the Americans treated us. They are a generous people and they gave us their hospitality without stint. But it was very interesting to see the difference between their attitude to the war and that of our men.

The Americans were green – greener than the greenest grass. They knew this and they knew that our men were old hands and they wanted to hear about the war from people who knew it from personal experience.

But the stories they wanted to hear were stories out of the Boys Own Paper – gallant officers waving gleaming swords as they led their brave men in glorious charges – noble soldiers cradling their dying comrades in their arms as they listened to the last whispered message to Mother – and so on. They just had no shadow of an idea what war was like.

As for our men, they had struggled and lived in everlasting mud; they had been gassed and blown up and wounded; they had been home and come out again to the same mud and filth; the war had been going on since the beginning of time and appeared to be going on for ever and ever; they had given up all hope of its ever ending and it was beyond their understanding that anyone should want to talk about it.

The Americans couldn't understand this utter weariness about the war and the two sides never got together – they just didn't talk the same language and the incomprehension was mutual.

About other things than the war, our men were also lethargic and uninterested. The Americans put on a base-ball game for us.

Our men referred to it scornfully as 'rounders' and thought that the traditional barracking of the umpire was just bad manners. I suppose this was partly due to insularity, but in an even larger degree to exhaustion. Our men were just fagged out and had not got the mental energy to cope with an entirely alien point of view.

Despite the fact that they speak a superficially similar language, the Americans are a foreign nation with a foreign outlook on life and it does take a considerable amount of mental energy to adjust to their point of view. I must say the Americans made a better attempt to adjust to and appreciate our point of view than we did to appreciate theirs. I hope it was only due to fatigue on our side, but, whatever the reason, the two sides did not really understand each other or get on together.

After a few days in the American camp we set out to find our various units. The RB were right back near the mouth of the Somme at a little place called Gamaches. (Inevitably 'Gamages' to the troops).

It must be understood that all this time that I had been wandering about France, I had not been in touch with my own battalion at all. They knew that I had arrived in the transport lines the day before the balloon went up and the QM would have been able to tell them that I had been sent up the line with a scratch mob on the night of 27th May. Since that date they had not heard from me or about me and so had, quite reasonably, reported me as 'Missing'. I don't know how long it was that my people had to wait before they heard that I was all right, but it must have been the best part of a month.

My Divisional History says that the casualties of the RB in the three days 27th to 30th May were 28 Officers and 744 Other Ranks. I can hardly believe this because an infantry battalion normally consists of 4 companies of 4 platoons of about 50 men each, which makes a total of 800 men. Add HQ staff, transport, signallers and other odds and ends and you might get a total of 1000 men. Similarly, 1 Company Commander and 4 platoon commanders to each company would add up to 20 officers. Add the CO; Adjutant QM; Transport Officer, Signal Officer, MO, and other odds and ends you might get a total of 30 officers at the outside. And this is only the nominal establishment. In actual fact, we never had as many as five officers to a company as far as I can remember. It was more usually two or three. At that late stage of the war, infantry battalions were never up to establishment, even allowing for the odd bodies away on leave or on courses. (John Terraine says that the 8th Division was reduced to a total ration strength of 1,500 men. Full establishment ration strength of a division is about 20,000)

I very much doubt if the battalion could have mustered more than 800 men, all told, when the show opened, so the official figures would mean that we had pretty nearly one hundred per cent casualties. I think the explanation must be that a large proportion of those shewn as casualties were in fact taken prisoners or were wandering about on their own like I was and were posted as missing. Of course, such people are casualties as far as the Army is concerned, but, for the individual, it is not nearly so bad to be taken prisoner or be missing. With luck, you can still have a life to lead after the war. But in places like Ypres or Passchendaele, casualties were nearly all killed or smashed up for good, which is much worse. This retreat had its sticky moments, but on the whole was not nearly so alarming or dangerous as the battles of the last half of 1917.

We must have had the best part of a month by the sea at Gamaches. We did some fairly strenuous training, but we lived comfortably and I was able to re-equip myself. I bought an American Army issue Gillette Safety Razor and was impressed by the fact that the Americans had the sense to issue safety razors to their troops. We all used them, but the official British army issue was the old cut-throat type, which is a good weapon for hooligans in back alleys, but not a very convenient shaving implement on active service. Safety razors were in general civilian use well before 1914; I should like to know how long it took before they became the official army issue.

We were only about ten miles from the little sea-side resort of Le Tréport and one day another fellow and myself got a day off and went to look at it. We went there on the foot plate of an engine; I cannot remember why, but I am sure it was not a legal means of transport. The engine driver said he dared not take us into the town, but there was some sand piled up alongside the track about a mile short of the station and he would slow down there and we were to jump off. He did slow down, but apparently was going a good deal faster than we realised, because we both came croppers and turned head over heels and got sand in our eyes and ears and up our noses and down our shirts. However, no bones were broken and we went on into the town on foot. We had a picnic lunch on the sands, grapes and warm champagne, and made friends with a fat French tradesman and his wife, who had two charming children.

We shared our champagne with Ma and Pa and our grapes with the children and then built sand-castles with them while their parents snoozed in deck-chairs. Then we had a good dinner in a hotel and made what we hoped were fool-proof arrangements for getting home again. There was a General dining at the same hotel and we found out that he had a car and would be going back along the Gamaches road later in the evening. We found his chauffeur and tipped him to keep his eyes open for us along the road and suggest to his boss that we might be given a lift. Unless he was in a very surly temper, the General would not be likely to refuse a lift to two officers plodding along a country road late at night.

We set off well before the General, hoping to be picked up within the first few miles, but there was one place where the road divided, because of road alterations or something, and while we were walking along one loop, we saw the car which must have been the General's, going along the other. And that was the only car we saw the whole night. We had to walk the whole ten or twelve miles and, though we arrived in time for early parade, we were pretty bleary-eyed and weary.

Another incident was a big field-day towards a deserted part of the coast, culminating with a final charge up the sand-dunes to attack an imaginary enemy who was supposed to have just landed. The first line of troops went up to the top of the sand-dunes and a brisk rattle of musketry broke out. When I came up to the top, with the second line, I found that everyone was enthusiastically firing at a couple of coasting barges that were making their way along the coast about half a mile out to sea. The troops were enjoying themselves, but as we were using live ammunition, the

The photographs on pages 149–52 are taken from a film in the Imperial War Museum. Probably filmed in 1918, the exact date and place of the film has not been established; it shows a day with the 2nd Rifle Brigade, and the author appeared in the film.

The author is third from the left, facing the camera.

barges were not. The sea all round them was pitted with little fountains and they were waving and shouting. We could not hear what they were saying, but it was obviously not a psalm of praise for their gallant allies. The troops thought it such fun, that we had quite a lot of difficulty in stopping the firing.

I nearly got killed here too, although we were so far from the front. I was walking across some marshes with another fellow. There was nobody about but some French officers behind a barn, a long way on our left. They waved and shouted at us, but we could not hear what they said and we waved back in friendly fashion and walked on. Suddenly there was a vicious whizz-bang and a shell burst a good deal less than a hundred yards in front. We looked back to see where it had come from, and saw a battery of French 75s on the ridge behind us. It appeared that we were walking right up their firing range, though we could not see any targets. They must have seen us, but they carried on firing just the same. In a case like this, the thing to do is to go sideways. A shell can easily drop short or over but the margin of error in a lateral direction is very much smaller so we turned at right angles to the line of fire and ran for it.

But although this holiday by the sea was very pleasant, it didn't seem to me that the battalion was quite the same. There was hardly anybody left that I knew. Even Alldridge, the QM, had got himself a 'blighty'. And the men were all mixed up and had come from all sorts of different units. I suppose the shortage of man-power was so great that they just had to get men where they could find them, but men who had been out before were disgruntled to find themselves pitched into strange regiments and missed their pals. It may have been unavoidable but it destroyed the esprit-de-corps. Also we were now getting a lot of men conscripted under the Derby Acts* who had been taken against their will and who had no esprit-de-corps anyway. At the time I felt that the battalion had deteriorated but now I see that I had probably deteriorated too. Ypres and Passchendaele had taken a lot out of me and I was not the man I used to be. I didn't realise it then, but I know now that I was more frightened and not so good at my job in the last

* Introduced by Lord Derby, these preceded formal conscription.

four months of the war. I daresay nobody was and the only consolation was that the Boche were also getting pretty tired of the war.

XI

The Last Lap

We entrained again for the front on 19th July. I was sent on ahead of the battalion with the billeting party. We travelled in a train with the 2nd East Lancs and detrained at a siding on the St Pol-Arras line at 5 a.m. on the 20th. It was light, but very misty and the East Lancs were starting to unload their transport, when a Boche plane, with its engine shut off, suddenly appeared out of the mist only about 50 feet up and flew all along the siding machine-gunning us. Everybody rushed for cover, but there wasn't any.

Being machine-gunned from the air was a commonplace in the second war, but we had not come across it before, at least in the open. Occasionally a plane would come along and strafe the front-line but that wasn't very dangerous. You were in a trench and the enemy plane never stayed very long because of fear of our fighters. But this thing coming out of the mist as silently as an owl and catching us all unawares was very alarming. The East Lancs had to stay and unload their train, but we didn't, so I gathered my little party together and we marched out down the road and had our breakfast in comfort under a hedge.

We went first to camps in the triangle Acq, Villers-au-Bois, Mont St Eloi, north-west of Arras and after two or three days took over a stretch of the line in front of Vimy Ridge. This front was a fairly active one, but we were much helped by the fact that we held the Ridge, which gave us observation over a large area of country, almost as far as Douai, fifteen miles to the east. The front line was down on the level, a couple of miles or so beyond the Ridge, but the Boche could only observe our activities from ground level, whereas we could sit on the Ridge and see every movement in his lines and for a long way behind them.

We made use of this advantage to harass the enemy as much as possible and this activity gave me the best day's sport I had during the war. I was given a 3 inch field-gun and told to make as much of a nuisance of myself as I could. I had organised a good deal of sniping at various times, but only with rifles. I had never before been out sniping with a field gun and I doubt whether many people ever had such an opportunity – certainly not many infantry men. The gun was commanded by an RA subaltern. It was his job to do the technical calculations and get his gun firing on the targets that I selected. I do not know how much damage we did, but we had a lot of fun.

I remember that late in the afternoon we were up in the roof of a ruined church, looking with our glasses through holes in the roof, when we spotted a Boche staff car going along a road that lay parallel to the front. The chance of tickling up some fat Boche staff officers was too good to be missed and we chased the car with shells for a mile or more. We didn't actually hit it but I think we got close enough to worry the occupants because, shortly after it had escaped in a burst of speed, the Boche artillery started retaliating on us and we had to climb down from our perch and pull out.

When the battalion was in Brigade reserve, we had a most marvellous dug out for Battalion HQ. It was dug into the steep eastern slope of the ridge and had a small verandah built out in front, where we used to eat breakfast, looking out for miles over the plain. It was like living in a Swiss chalet stuck up on the side of one of the Alps. When the Boche made it, it must have been an ideal spot, sheltered both from fire and observation. But now it was on the side of the hill facing the enemy, so we had to be careful not to show, by a lot of coming and going, that it was being used as an HQ. One morning, as we were breakfasting on our verandah, a single field gun planted itself on the top of the ridge behind us and started pooping off over our heads. Our CO was furious and went out himself to drive it away. The gunner officer was very young and green and did not know how to handle the situation. He said he was only carrying out orders that he had received, but our CO was not going to have our pleasant retreat brought to the enemy's notice, and he pulled his rank outrageously. He told the unfortunate subaltern to take himself and his blasted pop-gun away forthwith or he would be arrested and the poor boy crawled away with his tail between his legs. I was sorry for him; he was only doing what I had been doing a few days before. But self-preservation is one of the major instincts and I agreed with our CO's action, though the young man's only fault was that he had chosen his position unwisely.

The trench-mortar people were always making themselves unpopular in this sort of way. They would set up their gun in your part of the line, poop off a few rounds and then pack up and clear out, leaving you to suffer the inevitable retaliation. So whenever you found the trench-mortar people in your part of the line, you always hounded them out as quickly as possible and they had to wander about till they found a spot where there was no infantry officer in sight or only a young and green one.

When one got out of the line, there were comfortable hutted camps in the area round Acq and Villers-au-Bois and it was here that we came across our first tanks – active ones, that is, though we had seen plenty of abandoned ones stuck in the mud up at Ypres. One evening, we were all at dinner in one of the camps in this area, when the Boche started dropping long range shells into the camp. They were only coming over at about one a minute, but the second or third that arrived went right into a hut holding a hundred men or more. Luckily, it went down into the earth floor and failed to explode. There were only, I think, two casualties, but the CO decided to evacuate the camp. Officers were told to go down to their companies and take them out and bivouac in the woods around the camp. I was acting adjutant at the time and I was told to wait in the HQ hut with a couple of signallers.

I didn't like it, because it was a bit nerve-racking waiting for the next shell to arrive, but the signallers had to stay and someone had to stay with them. And it was a good thing I did stay, because within a quarter of an hour, Brigade rang up to say that they had had a report from another battalion that the Rifle Brigade had been seen streaming out of camp and what was it all about? I told them that we were being shelled, that the CO had decided to evacuate the camp and that the men had not 'streamed out', but had been marched out under their own company officers and that the CO had gone with them as was his job, but had left me to keep in touch and did the Brigadier want to speak to the CO personally, because if so, I would get him. I believe that the report that had been made represented us as fleeing out of camp in a panicking mob, but Brigade were relieved to find that everything was under control. The fact that someone had been left at the telephone to keep in touch at least showed that it was an ordered movement and not a panic dispersal.

Later that night I was relieved and went out into the woods, made myself a bivouac and went to sleep. Well before first light, I was woken up by all sorts of weird noises; coughs and snorts and rumblings like a herd of dinosaurs with tummy trouble. When I got up to investigate, I found there was a tank laager in the wood and they were warming up their engines and getting ready to go into the line further south. I did not dare to go to sleep again, I was terrified lest these snorting monsters would run over me and crush me to death in the dark. So I walked about and talked to the men and cadged some tea and even got a ride on one tank for a short distance when they moved off. But I was glad I was only a Poor Bloody Infantryman and did not have to go into battle in a rolling tin-can and suffer sea-sickness as well as all the other horrors of war.

Near here there was a big ruined church at Mont St Eloi. I was surprised to see it and said to a civilian that I did not know the Boche had ever got as far west as this. He explained that this church had not been destroyed in this war, but in 1870, and that made me think. 1870 to 1918 – only 48 years – twice in one man's lifetime this country had been ravaged by war. The Boche must be a nation of madmen to have unleashed this horror on the world twice in such a short time. They must obviously be slapped down and, like other raving lunatics, restrained so that they could not run amok again.

And that is what we thought we were doing. We were told that this was 'the war to end war' and some of us, at least, believed it. It may sound extraordinarily naive now, but then, I think, one had to believe it. All the mud and blood and bestiality only made sense on the assumption that it was the last time civilised men would ever have to suffer it. I could not believe that anyone who had been through it could ever allow it to happen again. I thought that the ordinary man on both sides would rise up as one and kick any politician in the teeth who even mentioned the possibility of another war.

I was wrong, of course. I knew something of the folly of mankind, but not enough. And I definitely had no idea how short people's memories were. If I live to be a hundred, which God forbid, the war will always be the central and most vivid part of my life and I did not realise that it was not so with everyone. But if I had known that it was all going to happen again within twenty-five years, I would have shot myself or, if I lacked the courage to do that, would have run, howling, away and been shot by others as a deserter.

After about a month in this part of the world, our division was ordered to take over a stretch of line further to the south. This was done by moving our brigade from the left of the divisional front and putting it into the new southern sector. I suppose this was better than making each of the three brigades side-step, but it meant, since we had to be in our new positions before dawn, that our relief in the northern sector had to take place in daylight. This would not have been too difficult in normal circumstances, as the communication trenches were good and movement right up to the front line was quite feasible in daylight. But what the staff overlooked was that the eastern side of Vimy Ridge was so steep that the enemy could see right into the communication trenches running down its eastern face from their own lines; much better, in fact, than they could see into the trenches closer to the line.

The relieving troops started to come down the front of the Ridge about three in the afternoon. The sun was shining brightly and the glint of sunlight on rifle barrels and bits of brass soon gave the show away. By the number of men coming in, the Boche must have known that a relief was in progress and they started shelling the whole area. I was just passing the first of the incoming troops in a brick-yard at the foot of the ridge when a 3-inch shell fell right in the middle of a platoon. It made a most ghastly mess and I was glad that it was not part of my job to stay and clear it up.

The reason that I was coming out of the line so early was that I had been detailed as 'embussing officer'. That meant that I had to go up to the rendezvous with the ASC lorries and dispatch the companies to their new destination as they came out of the line. We only had to go about five miles down towards Arras and normally we should have marched it. But on this occasion we were given lorries, because we had to take over our new positions and let the people we were relieving get out before dawn.

The lorries had been ordered to wait for the troops at the Vert-Tilleul crossroads. That was a damned silly spot to choose for a rendezvous. It was true that it was out of sight of the enemy, but crossroads were always chosen as targets for indirect harassing fire. You are much more likely to hit something where four roads meet than if you drop shells casually along any one of the roads.

So the first thing I did when I got there about four o'clock was to move the lorries about three hundred yards down the road towards Arras. Nothing happened from four till eight. The companies arrived one by one as they were relieved and were duly dispatched to their destinations. It wasn't until the HQ Section of the battalion were just appearing over the crest of the hill that the Boche started shelling. The men started to move to the sides of the road to get what little cover the banks afforded but the CO called them back and made them march in the middle of the road. That seemed to me absurd. It is true that the banks were low and would only have afforded protection from one direction, but even that seems to me to be worth taking when you are under shell fire. And nothing whatever was gained by making them march in fours in the middle of the road, except that it satisfied the regular army's sense of parade ground discipline, to be adhered to in all circumstances.

But I had not long to consider the deficiencies of the regular army's methods, because a stray shell suddenly came in our direction. It passed through the canvas cover of the lorry I was standing by, luckily without hitting the iron supports for the cover, and burst on the far side of the road. The HQ party, from a hundred yards up the road, were certain that I had been killed, so the CO told me when he arrived. The Boche were using a high-velocity naval gun, but my velocity was higher and I swear I was in the ditch on my side of the road before the shell exploded on the other.

The rest of the night was without any particular incident and, by dawn, we found ourselves in the line somewhere in front of Roclincourt, just north of the Scarpe.

It was here that a new padre joined us. We did not have a padre all the time; they came and went. I think I can remember four during the time I was with the RB. Most of them were not bad fellows in their way, but they all seemed to me entirely useless. I may be hopelessly prejudiced and they may have been of use to somebody. All I can say is that it didn't come to my attention.

But this new chap was worse than useless. We had a reasonably comfortable dug-out for Battalion HQ with wire bunks and a table. It was very crowded of course; but dug-outs always were, with the HQ officers and their batmen, the signallers and other odds and ends. This was better than most, but when the padre learned that his accommodation was a share in a bunk, when someone else wasn't using it, and a seat on a box at the table, he took me aside and, quite seriously, said that he could not be expected to live in those conditions and he must have a place apart where he could 'meditate'.

I am afraid I was not very sympathetic. It was probably more ignorance than arrogance, but it seemed strange to me that, as late as the summer of 1918, anyone could be so ignorant of the conditions that we had all got so used to. And a few days later, he annoyed me by coming in full of self-praise and telling me how he had been right round the front line giving cigarettes to the 'dear men'. That anyone should think that a stroll up to the front line in good trenches on a quiet day and in daylight should be a matter for self-congratulation was beyond me. It did not seem to occur to him that the 'dear men' that he had so daringly visited had to live in the line day and night in all conditions and had no comfortable dug-out to retire to if things got noisy.

I don't think I should have minded so much if he had been just a fool. But for such a fool to set himself up as our spiritual adviser and demand special privileges to allow him to 'meditate' in comfort got under my skin.

There were other incidents that shewed this man up in an unfavourable light, but the thing that really set me against parsons as a race was the sort of notice that used to appear in 'Orders' when we were in Richmond Park. 'There will be a voluntary Church Parade to-morrow at 11.00 hrs. B Coy will supply 1 officer and 50 men.' How any parson could allow that I could not understand.

If the CO wanted a well-attended church parade and ordered people to attend, the padre couldn't stop him. But he could have seen that it was not called a 'voluntary' parade. Even in those early days, I decided that a church that was so spineless was not worth bothering about and nothing I saw of it in the war, or since, has given me reason to change my mind. I daresay there may be some good in it somewhere if one looks for it and I admit that I haven't bothered to look. It seems to me too much like looking for a needle in a haystack. And that is a long and wearisome job, particularly if you don't happen to want a needle.

And while on the subject of odd characters, it is worth while mentioning our doctor. He was extremely brave and that is definitely a virtue in war-time, however much intellectuals may denigrate it as 'mere physical courage' and he devoted himself to the wounded without thought for his own safety or comfort. But he got himself into trouble with the authorities whenever he went on leave because he was always, from their point of view, improperly dressed. He was, of course, a member of the RAMC but he was so devoted to the Rifle Brigade that he dressed as much like a rifleman as possible, wearing a black tie, as we did, and even blacking his RAMC buttons and cap-badge.

He also carried a small camera and took pictures of the war as it really was. I should very much like to have done that too, and could have made a record that would have been intensely interesting personally and possibly valuable historically. But it was a court-martial offence to carry a camera and I was too frightened to risk it. The doctor could not, of course, send his rolls of film home to be developed through the post, so he used to get people going on leave to take them for him. I did it for him once, but I was terrified all the time until I got rid of it.

Sometime in 1917, I think it might have been at Ypres, he got the base-plate of a shell all to himself. It smashed his jaw and all the lower part of his face to a jelly and for months he had to be fed through a straw. But he recovered and I believe was patched up satisfactorily, though he never came back to us.

Of his successors, the only one who has made any impression on my memory was an American, attached to us from the American army to learn about the war at first-hand. I shared a hut with him once and, first thing in the morning, he used to clear his throat and expectorate lavishly all over the floor. It struck me as an unhygienic practice, especially for a doctor.

During this summer, the Army had one of its brain-waves and decided that a certain number of people should be attached, for short periods, to other arms, so that each could learn something about the other fellow's point of view. It was a good idea, in general, that one half should see how the other half lived, but the particular aspect that appealed to me was that it produced additional opportunities of getting short spells out of the line. It gave me two or three days with an 8 inch howitzer battery and a whole week with the Flying Corps.

The days with the gunners were not particularly comfortable. Although they were a good way behind the line, they still had to live in dug-outs. And though they did not get shelled as frequently as the PBI, when they did, it was with heavy stuff. I did not like things that went bang and the louder the bang, the less I liked it. You could hear a heavy howitzer shell rumbling and grumbling through the air like an express train for about a week before it arrived and I always bolted underground if one sounded as though it was coming anywhere near the battery position. But the artillerymen seemed to know to a yard where it was going to land and never moved unless the thing dropped practically into their laps. I envied their sang-froid but did not attempt to match it. On the other hand, I have taken a party of artillerymen up to forward positions and had them ducking and spreading all over the place under machine-gun fire, although the bullets were going miles over our heads. Which merely serves to show that the Devil you know is less terrifying than the Devil you don't know and that you can come to terms with anything.

But the week with the Flying Corps was a real holiday. We lived in huts well beyond the range of shell fire, slept in real beds with sheets, ate in a proper mess and could have a hot bath every day. It was the infantryman's dream of Paradise. But I don't think

I could have left all that luxury and gone off before dawn to fight a lone battle in the sky as they did. I think that took more courage than just sitting in the mud and waiting to be killed by accident.

I learned something about the interpretation of aerial photography, a science that was then only in its infancy and I managed to get a ride in an aeroplane. These were still of the 'stick and string' variety and aerodromes were only levelled fields, so merely to go up was quite an adventure. When I asked the Adjutant for permission, he refused. But, later, in the mess, he said to me: 'You chaps that come here for visits are all mad to fly, but if I let you go up and you get killed, I get blamed. Therefore, I will not give you permission. But if you can find a pilot who is willing to take you and I don't know anything about it and you don't kill yourself, then nothing will be said.'

So I set about looking for a pilot who would take me up. The man I found had already crashed two planes that day and was being sent up for the third time on the principle that, if you fall off a horse, you must mount and ride again so that you do not lose your nerve.

I thought he was going to crash a third plane, because we ran right across the aerodrome and only got our wheels off the ground inches before the edge of a ploughed field. But, once up, it was lovely. I don't suppose we flew at more than sixty miles an hour, but the wind singing through the wires and against your face in the open cock-pit gave you much more sensation of speed than you get boxed up in a modern air liner flying ten times as fast.

Our sole armament was a Lewis gun, mounted on a rail that encircled the observer's seat. Every time I got up to look over the side at something of particular interest, the butt of this damned gun swung round and hit me in the stomach and knocked me back into my seat. It was a good job we did not meet an enemy fighter, as I don't think I should have been an effective gunner. The pilot had no particular job to do and he took me over Vimy Ridge, over ground that I knew well. It was impressive to see the roads on our side crawling with traffic, while, on the Boche side, nothing moved for several miles back. We went right over and beyond the Boche lines, far enough to attract anti-aircraft fire, but that did not worry us.

In case that sounds unduly boastful, it must be explained that anti-aircraft gunnery was still in a very primitive stage. There were none of the modern electronic devices; you just pointed the gun at where you hoped the aeroplane might be some seconds later and let fly. The percentage of failures was so high that 'Archie' was regarded as a joke. When I looked over the side of the plane at the shell-bursts below us, I can honestly say that I was only interested and not in the least alarmed. I think this must have been the only occasion in the whole war when I was under shell fire without being frightened half out of my wits.

Other amusements that I was introduced to that summer were court martials. I had attended some before but only as a learner. That meant that one sat through the whole trial, except the private deliberation on verdict and sentence, and was asked one's idea of what a suitable sentence would be. Junior officers were asked first, so that their opinions would not be influenced by those of their seniors and the ideas of appropriate sentences varied wildly – from twenty years to six months in one case. Of course, these proposals had no influence on the decision of the court itself; they were only asked for to make the learners attend to the evidence and use their heads.

I first got interested in legal procedure when I had to make a precis of the evidence for a Court of Inquiry in a case where a man had been shot in the stomach during Lewis gun drill. The squad had been sitting in a barn, taking it in turns to practise setting up the gun, putting on the tray of ammunition, cocking the gun and pressing the trigger. The tray was filled with dummy cartridges of wood; they were quite different from live cartridges in both weight and appearance and it would seem to be impossible that even a blind man could have accidentally slipped a live round in with the dummies when loading the tray. Moreover, this was a special tray, kept for drill purposes only, that had been used dozens of times before without an accident. And there was no evidence of malice aforethought. The man who actually pressed the trigger was the wounded man's best friend and was terribly upset at what he had done. It all seemed quite insoluble to me, but I was not a member of the Court and I forget what their verdict was.

I was impressed with the general fairness of the court martial procedure. The commander of an army in the field obviously has to be given wide powers to deal with a variety of offences, but in the actual trial a great effort is made to give the prisoner every possible assistance and he is given the benefit of any possible doubt. In fact, everyone leans over backwards to make sure that the prisoner's case is not prejudiced.

I once got a man off on the technicality that, as Prisoner's Friend, I had not had the requisite 48 or 72 (or whatever the statutory figure was) hours in which to consult him and prepare the case. The whole affair was quite simple. The prisoner was a first class soldier in the line, brave and reliable and worth his weight in gold, according to his CO's report. But out of the line, he was a menace whenever he could get hold of drink. I think, on this occasion, he had burnt down a barn and endangered a whole farm. There was not much doubt about the facts and there was no point in disputing them. The only line of defence would have been to stress his good qualities when in the line. But the technical point I brought up about my not having had the statutory period of notice was accepted by the Court, not because they thought that there would have been any real chance of my producing fresh evidence or even preparing my case more efficiently, but simply because the prisoner might have been deprived, ever so slightly, of getting the best defence available to him and he was entitled to the benefit of the doubt.

The whole question of punishment was bedevilled by the fact that the war was so bloody. Punishments for minor offences that the Army called crimes, but which were not generally considered as such in civil life, were confined to loss of privileges, such as CB and extra fatigues. There were no barracks to which one could be confined anyway and fatigues were universal. The most serious punishment a battalion commander could inflict was Field Punishment No. 1. This meant being tied, spread-eagled, to a wagon wheel for a specified number of hours. A lot of hot air has been talked about the iniquity of this, but I cannot see that it was so terrible. You were not lashed tightly to the wagon wheel; you were never kept there for more than an hour at a time; you were loosed if it got too hot or too cold or if it rained, so there was very little physical discomfort. Presumably, it was the moral effect that was supposed to be the deterrent. This might have been effective in civil life, when 'What will the neighbours think' is an important influence. But here, the neighbours were the man's own mates and they thought it was just a bit of bad luck, carrying no disgrace whatever.

After all, there was such a lot of bad luck about, hitting the just and the unjust indiscriminately, that one did not blame a man when he got caught by it. And a few hours No 1 was such a minor piece of bad luck compared to the chance of getting killed or mutilated that everyone was taking all the time, that it really did not seem very important.

It must be remembered that we were not soldiers, but civilians in uniform. We were in the Army but not of it. What the Army thought of us did not matter. What did matter was what they did to us. And nothing that they dared to do to us behind the lines was anything like as bad as the ordinary conditions in the line, so the powers of the authorities were to some extent limited.

This was exemplified in the treatment of the more serious crimes that were dealt with by general court martials (as opposed to field court martials). These courts could sentence men to some years of imprisonment in Army prisons. By all accounts, these 'glass-houses' were pretty tough places, which one would normally take a good deal of trouble to avoid. But the conditions in the worst of the military prisons were so much better than conditions in the line that the authorities found that they were getting lumbered up with people who had deliberately committed serious crimes in order to get out of the line and into the comparative comfort of a nice warm prison.

The answer to that was the 'suspended sentence'. You got your two or five years or whatever it was, but this sentence was suspended till after the war and the criminal was sent straight back into the line. Even officers who were cashiered were immediately conscripted and sent out again, to another regiment, as private soldiers.

This was effective. But it is an illuminating commentary on the conditions of the times that no punishment that the authorities dared to inflict was worse than the ordinary day-to-day life in the line.

I have not said much about the Flying Corps, because the ordinary infantry man did not have much to do with it. During a big show, certain planes would be detailed for 'Contact Patrol' work, which meant flying low over the battle area to try and find out how far the forward troops had progressed. This was a nasty job because when an attack was in progress, both sides were hurling tons of metal at each other and to fly low through this was more dangerous than any amount of the primitive Ack-Ack fire. The forward troops carried flares with which to notify their position, but it usually seemed that there was no contact patrol plane visible when you had time to think about flares or that, when a plane did appear, the man with the flares had got lost. This was the only time when you had, consciously, to watch for planes.

But what was exciting was the individual battles between planes. Fighter planes were mostly armed with fixed machine guns firing through the propeller, so that to aim your gun, you had to aim your plane itself at the enemy. The killing position was to dive on your enemy's tail and everyone tried to manoeuvre his plane into this position, while the other fellow, of course, tried to prevent your doing so. And all this was not just indicated by streaks in the sky miles above your head. It was mostly at low altitudes, where you could see everything that was happening and follow every twist and turn. And the way they twisted and turned and threw their planes about the sky was truly terrifying. It did not seem that any plane could stand the strain. Sometimes, of course, they did not and broke up in the air, but you had to take a chance on that. The alternative was a machine-gun bullet in your back or your petrol tank and that gave you no chance at all. The acrobatics that took place in actual fighting were ten times more hair-raising than any that have ever been put on in an air show.

I remember watching a fight in which the Englishman seemed to be getting the worst of it. Time and again the Boche got on his tail and the Englishman only escaped by desperate turning and side-slipping at the last possible moment. And all the time he was losing height and with it, his room for manoeuvre. Finally, when he was only about twenty feet above the ground, he flattened out and made for home. I imagine he thought he was done for and had decided that, if he had to be shot down, he would try and fall on his own side of the line. One could almost see the Boche's grin of triumph as he made his final dive on to the Englishman's tail.

But just then a machine-gun opened up from the ground and the Boche plane crashed in flames right under our eyes. It looked for all the world as though the Englishman had been luring the Boche on and had deliberately led him right over the machine-gun nest. I don't think that is possible, because the British pilot could not have known that there was a machine-gun nest just in that position, but that is what it looked like.

Other people who had to fight a lonely war all by themselves were the people in the observation balloons. They went up from well behind the lines, but sometimes the Boche would select one for a little target practice. The men had no defence except to ask to be pulled down and that was a slow job, giving the Boche plenty of time to alter the elevation of his guns and go on potting at the balloon as it descended. Occasionally, a daring spirit would have his balloon sent higher so that the next shell burst well below him. But that was not a game one could play for long. There is not much scope for dodging if you can only move straight up or down.

One of the nastier incidents of this sort that I saw was when the Boche was particularly annoyed with one balloon and sent over a plane to put it down. We saw the plane circle the balloon and fire at it and we saw the little line of flame where the bullets hit. The only thing the observer can do in a case like this is to get out and that is what he did. We saw him fall and we saw his parachute open safely. The Boche plane did not return and fire at the man, as they sometimes did, but streaked for home and it seemed that the incident had ended happily.

But as the balloon burnt it started to fall faster. It was a dead still day and we could see the man hanging from his parachute, while the flaming mass of the balloon fell faster and faster down on to him. I only hope that he could not see what we could see. It is possible that the parachute might have prevented him from seeing what was going on directly over his head; then he would not have known anything until the balloon caught him up and burnt his parachute in a flash and he would have fallen to a fairly quick and merciful death. But I only hope it was like that; I don't know.

XII

Enemy in Retreat

But I have digressed since I left the battalion in the Roclincourt sector. This must have been about the middle of August. The main advance had already begun to the south of us on the other side of the Scarpe. We did not do any big show north of the Scarpe but there was a good deal of probing to test the enemy's resistance and small advances where opportunity offered. As part of the general probing, I was told to take out a patrol from a sap that led out of our front line. I had just got out of the sap and was working through our own wire, when the Boche let loose a salvo of trench-mortar bombs that fell all round the end of the sap. I must have been knocked out for a moment or two and I can't think why I wasn't killed.

The men in the sap were sure I had been hit and the first thing I heard when I came to was somebody saying, 'Well, I suppose we had better go and bring him in.' Then someone else said, 'Yes. Let's go now before the next lot come over.'

I had recovered sufficiently by that time to tell them to stay in the sap, but I thought it pretty good of the men to be prepared to come out and fetch me. The obvious thing to do was to withdraw to the main line and nobody would have blamed them for doing so. In fact, that is what we did as soon as I had crawled back into the sap. The men concerned in this incident did not know me personally and I did not know them; it was just that we were members of the same battalion – a good one.

By the end of August the advance on our right had spread up to and across the Scarpe and it became necessary for us to get forward in order to cover the flank of the division on our right. There was a good deal of quite heavy fighting round Oppy Wood and the village of Gavrelle. We lost our CO on 24th September and Roger Brand came back and resumed command of the battalion, but only for a very short time as he was soon promoted to brigadier and took over our own, the 25th, Brigade. But I cannot remember any of the detail of this time until we had got beyond both the Rouvroy–Fresnes line and the Drocourt–Queant line. That marked the end of trench warfare and I remember how we all stood up and cheered as the 2nd Berkshires came through us at Quiery-la-Motte, marching in fours with all the text-book apparatus of an advance-guard in front and the CO riding at the head of his battalion. This was in the early part of October and, though we had still some way to go, it was the first faint glimmer of hope that the war might be going to have an end to it sometime.

During this advance we suffered a good deal from booby-traps. In every planned retreat the Boche always left trouble behind him in some form. On the Somme, the 2nd Devons lost nearly half their officers when a farm-house that they were using as an officers' mess blew up. This was due to a delayed-action mine – one of those things that is set off by acid eating through a wire. So we were not unprepared, but now the Boche seemed to concentrate on smaller things – a *pickelhaube*, for instance, hanging on a wall, that exploded when a souvenir hunter tried to take it down. I was sent to explore some dug-outs in a big railway embankment in front of Quiery-la-Motte with a Canadian RE sergeant, to see if they were safe for the battalion to use. This Canadian's methods of testing for booby-traps were most alarming. He would go up to any suspicious-looking object, e.g. a wire sticking out of a wall, and give it a tug, while I stood outside the doorway and implored him to be careful. I presume he knew what he was doing, since he did not blow us both up, but it did not look like it and I found going round with him a nerve-racking experience.

The Boche dug-outs that we were investigating were, of course, on the eastern side of the embankment with their openings towards the Boche and he was shelling the area methodically with heavy stuff – 8 inch howitzers. The shells were only arriving singly, at about one a minute, and the drill was that, when we had finished inspecting one dug-out, we would wait for the next shell and, as soon as it had exploded, make a dash for the next dug-out. But it was pitch dark and we did not know how far along the next dug-out might be, so it was a chancy business. At one time, we heard a shell rumbling through the sky like an express train, but we could not find another dug-out and it was too far to go back to the one we had just left. We ran like hares, but it wasn't until the last minute that we saw an extra black piece of darkness that seemed as though it might be an entrance and dived into it. Unfortunately, it was not the entrance to a dug-out but only to a small wooden shed. The shell exploded alongside and blew the shed down on top of us. We were not hurt, but I got two small pieces of metal in my leg and shoulder.

After we had finished the job, I went to the aid post and got the doctor to have a look at me. He probed about a bit, but could not find anything and, in fact, the wounds did not give me any trouble at all. But the doctor insisted that I should report myself as 'wounded', in case they turned septic. I was acting as adjutant at the time and personally wrote out the casualty signal and I was careful to report myself as 'Wounded, at duty'. This is army language to indicate that a man has been wounded, but so slightly that he is remaining on duty. It is a silly expression, because, if the commas get omitted, as they are likely to do in transmission, it reads that one is 'wounded at duty' and everybody is on duty when he gets wounded. Therefore my efforts to spare my people unnecessary anxiety were fruitless and they just got the official notification that I had been wounded, without any qualification, and had to wait till they got a field post-card from me before they knew that it was nothing to worry about.

Having got my name into the official casualty list, however, I was entitled to put up a wound stripe, but I did not have the cheek to do so.

At this time, the Boche was getting pushed back both north and south of us, but he made a stand at Douai, which was protected by a canal that ran along the West side of the town. This was a formidable obstacle and somebody in our Divisional Engineers evolved a scheme for getting troops across the canal on home-made rafts of duck-boards. A demonstration was held on a farm pond and all the big-wigs were there – the Divisional General, all three Brigadiers and various officers from battalions.

The rafts were supposed to support two men in full battle-kit and two unfortunate men were dressed up in all their gear and launched on the pond. But they had not paddled two strokes before the whole thing upset and they were pitched into the pond and had to be dragged out, covered in slime and cursing volubly. It was an amusing fiasco, enjoyed by all but the two men on the raft and the RE officer whose brain-child had so let him down.

Our battalion was a little to the north of Douai and, though there was a lot of shelling, we didn't have much actual fighting. In fact, there was only one serious battle, which was fought on 12th October by the East Lancs to take Douai prison and of which I had a good view from the north. The prison was a big building on the west of Douai with enormously thick walls, like a fort, and the East Lancs had a sticky time taking it. After it was taken, there was the canal to cross, which would have been difficult to do under fire, so we more or less marked time, hoping that the Boche would be forced to evacuate Douai by pressure on both the north and south and that we should not have to fight our way through the town and this is what did actually happen.

I set up an observation post on the roof of a château near the canal from which we could see a Boche sentry-group in the garden of a house on the other side. One morning, 17th October, very early, my observers reported that the sentry-group wasn't there any more and I went haring back to Battalion HQ to tell them that I thought the Boche had gone. The CO decided to send out a patrol to see if it was true and I went up to the forward company with the message and then on with the platoon that was detailed to do the patrol. We found a bridge that had been blown up so that it had collapsed in the middle, but it was possible for men to scramble along the girders to the bottom of the V, where the bridge rested in the canal, and up the other side. The platoon commander lined his men up along the bank of the canal to give covering fire and sent one section across the broken bridge with orders to spread out and form a small bridge-head on the other side. When this had been done without opposition, he passed his other sections over one by one and enlarged the bridge-head. I waited till the platoon commander himself went over and then I sent a message back that we were actually in Douai. After doing this, I went along the near bank of the canal to find out what was happening on our right.

I was pretty sure that the Boche had withdrawn, at least to the other side of the canal, if not further, or I would not have gone down the tow path by myself. But, even so, I got the fright of my life when, as we were passing a cottage a good half mile down the bank, we heard the clatter of breaking crockery. My runner unslung his rifle and I drew my revolver and, in great trepidation, we crept up the garden path as quietly as we could. Then we flung open the door and rushed in -- to be confronted with a tiny kitten who was crawling about on the dresser from which he had knocked down a cup. The relief was so great that we both burst out laughing to think how frightened we had been of such a harmless little object.

A little further on I found the 2nd Royal Berks crossing another broken bridge as we had done, so I went back to our own advanced patrol to tell them what was going on and back to get further troops sent across the canal. Then I wrote up a proper text-book report on the state of the canal bank and the places where it could be crossed. I doubt if it was ever read by anybody or would have been much use if it had been, but I felt I had to do it, because it was so seldom that one had the chance to carry out, in actual warfare, any of the academic exercises one learnt in training.

Douai was evacuated without any fighting and, as far as the buildings themselves were concerned, the town was more or less intact. But inside the buildings everything of value had been removed and everything else wantonly smashed and destroyed. Not only things that might have been of some use to us, but everything – mirrors, furniture, pictures, crockery, even the organ in the Cathedral, all smashed to atoms. Mattresses were ripped open and the stuffing scattered; even children's toys were broken up in a senseless orgy of destruction. I saw a French gendarme weeping openly as he looked at the wreck of his own home and held in his hands the remains of a broken doll. The damage done by modern warfare is appalling enough. There was absolutely no point in going to so much trouble to make it worse.

Here also, I saw the only incident I came across myself of deliberate cruelty. A cat had been put, alive, into a cavity in a brick wall and shut in with an iron grill. The cavity was just long enough for the cat to turn round in and when we found the poor brute it was gaunt with starvation. It tore at our men's hands through the grill as they laboured to dig out the ironwork with their bayonets and when it was released, it shot off and would not let anyone come near it even with food. This was an absolutely pointless piece of cruelty that we could not understand.

After Douai, the advance became swifter and the Boche more demoralised and there were signs that he was worse off than we were, which was a pleasant change. For example, wounded were found with bandages on them of paper only. And I remember examining one prisoner's gas-mask that had leather round the face-piece instead of rubber. That impressed me because if the leather got wet, it would go hard and would not fit closely round the contours of the face, so that the mask would be almost useless. Also, it became clear that the enemy were no longer controlling the pace of the retreat, but were being pushed back faster than they wanted to go. At one place, we found a château with a meal still on the table and a whole lot of fine glassware, all ready packed in cases for removal, which had had to be left behind.

But the enemy still had time to leave booby-traps. In this same château, we were all sitting round the fire after dinner – it was well into October by this time – when somebody suggested that the fire needed more coal. I was nearest the coal-scuttle so I picked it up and was just going to tip it on the fire, when I noticed some egg-bombs hidden in the coal. These were small black bombs of approximately the same size and shape as a hen's egg. They had obviously been hidden in the coal scuttle in the hope of catching somebody.

Another trick was to place one of the ordinary stick bombs under every fish-plate on the railway lines. This meant that one bomb buckled two lengths of rail and this was done the whole way up to Brussels, at least.

I can remember very little of the advance from Douai, except one incident when I was sent back to bring up the officers' horses. No bridges had yet been built across the canal and, though we had managed to get troops over by using the girders of blown-up bridges, there was no possibility of getting horses across them. There was, however, one place where there was a lock and the stone sills that carried the lock-gates jutted out from each bank and reduced the width of the canal by about half. Across this comparatively narrow gap, we put timbers from ruined cottages – roof beams and the like – and on top of these, doors and tables to make some sort of a surface.

The whole contraption was very rickety and the horses did not like it, but we had one mare with a placid temperament who took everything as it came and we led her backwards and forwards over the makeshift bridge to give the others confidence. In the end, we got them all over, under her leadership, but I had one moment of horror when the CO's own horse put a hind hoof through a door panel and started to panic. Fortunately, he lunged forward and was on the bank before he had time to start plunging about in other directions and his groom soon had him under control.

By 20th October we had got so far forward that we were finding civilians in the towns and villages that we occupied. They were, of course, pleased to see us, but were in a pretty bad way, most of them. The Boche did not deal kindly with civilians. I remember doing billeting at one farm where there was only an old couple, both over seventy, I should think. After they had shewn me what rooms were available, I thought to ask them where they themselves slept. They said they would lie on the tiled floor of the kitchen. I didn't like the idea of these two old people sleeping on the hard floor while young and healthy officers slept in their beds and said so. Their reply was: 'We always had to do it for the Boche; it will be less hardship to do it for you.' But they slept in their own beds that night.

One of the odd jobs that I had to do in this period was to round up the girls in the villages who had been unduly amiable to the Germans and take them to the MO for inspection. There was a rumour that the Germans had let loose VD patients from their hospitals when they saw the war was going against them, to infect as many people as possible, hoping that the disease would be passed on to our troops. I don't know whether this was true or not, but our authorities took the necessary precautions. There was no difficulty in identifying the girls. Their neighbours were only too willing to point them out.

We went up through Marchiennes and St Amand and were being held up along the line of the Scheldt River and the Canal du Jard when the division was relieved on the night of 4th/5th November and went back to the Marchiennes area. We were at dinner on the night of 5th November when an urgent signal came through that there was a leave vacancy for one officer if he could get down to rail-head within an hour. I can't remember where the rail-head was. It may have been Douai. Anyway, it was about ten miles away and it was going to be touch and go to get there in time for the train.

The Leave Roster was hurriedly produced, but all the men near the top of the list were away or sick or, for some reason, could not be got at without delay. It was unthinkable that a leave vacancy should be allowed to go by default and, as I was the man nearest the top of the list who was immediately available, I was told to make a dash for it. And dash I did, borrowing a bicycle from the Signallers and pedalling off into the darkness just as I got up from the table, in slacks and a tin hat. And I made it. I remember skittering over broken glass in the station and hurling myself into the train as it started, but I have no idea what happened to the bike.

The next day, going on board the leave ship, I had another bit of luck. I bumped into Roger Brand, presently brigadier of our brigade, but who had been in command of our battalion for most of the time I had been with it. He was a first-class chap and when he saw me he said: 'Oh, are you going on leave, Nettleton? Then you had better come and be my ADC.' I have no idea whether he had authority to have an ADC, but he was at least a general of sorts and no one questioned his right. Anyway, it was only a dodge to do me a good turn. I had no duties, but the appointment meant that I could not be snaffled for duty on the ship and that I went up in the first train from Folkestone with all the big-wigs. Roger Brand was like that. He could be a severe disciplinarian, but he looked after his men and we would all try to do anything he asked of us.

XIII

Armistice

When I left the battalion, people had said to me, 'It will all be over before you get back.' I did not believe them, but that is how it happened. November 11th was my birthday and the Armistice was the best birthday present any man ever had.

I went down to the Promenade at Cheltenham with my sister Mary and we saw all the people milling about in the streets and singing and dancing, but, even so, it was impossible to realise that the war, that had been going on since the beginning of time, was really over. I don't think I did realise it till I got on the leave train at Victoria to go back to France and found that it was just another railway journey. Always before, at seven o'clock in the morning, Victoria station had been a very grim place, with people wrapped up in their own private griefs and nobody taking any notice of anyone else. Now, it was just a railway station and the good-byes were 'Au revoirs' and not 'Adieux'.

I got 'flu on the way back to my battalion. I knew I had got it on the way up and ought to have reported sick. But I had heard a rumour that our division was going to Germany and I wanted to go with them, so I said nothing and went on. At rail-head, I found one of our limbers and got a ride back to the battalion. A limber is just a square box on wheels, without any springs, and a ride in one for ten miles over French cobbles with your head feeling as big as a football is not the best cure for influenza. However, I got to the village where the battalion was billeted and went to the Orderly Room to report my arrival. I made a vague attempt at a salute and then fell all over the Adjutant's desk. The MO was sent for and, within a quarter of an hour of my arrival, I was in an ambulance on my way to hospital. The battalion did not go to Germany after all, so I gained nothing by my efforts to re-join them.

Hospital was a new and interesting experience. It was only a field hospital. The wards were big marquees, but we had wooden floors and real beds, with sheets, and were quite comfortable. The sheets were rather horrifying to look at, being stained with blood and muck, but I argued that they had been washed and what had not come out in the wash would not come off on me. Anyway, I was too ill to be very finicky.

The nurses were magnificent and earned my undying admiration. And this was not altogether because we had been cut off from feminine company for so long that anything in a skirt seemed marvellous. There was some of that feeling, of course; but these girls were not only young and feminine, they knew their job and brought both skill and courage to it. Two instances will suffice.

One day a man was brought in suffering from concussion, due to a fall from a horse. When you have concussion, it appears that you lose control of your bodily functions and vomit and do everything else as a baby does, without volition or control. I did not know this but the nurses did. This man suddenly started to vomit. The nurse went over to him, put two fingers on one side of his chin, turned his head to the side and caught the vomit in a kidney dish held in her other hand. It was all done so neatly and cleanly that it was all over almost before I had properly realised what was happening. And yet there was no flapping or rushing about. The nurse didn't even appear to run. One moment she was going about her duties in the ward and the next she was at the man's bedside, coping completely competently with the situation. She must, of course, have been watching him closely all the time, but there was no sign of it in her demeanour. The whole thing was an example of expert skill – knowing exactly what to do and how to do it – that impressed me enormously. It was so different from the well-meaning, but clumsy, amateurism that one seems to come across so frequently in many walks of life.

The other incident concerned the man in the next bed to mine, who was very ill indeed. In the middle of the night, he suddenly became delirious. When the nurse went to him, he sat up in bed and gave her a tremendous punch in the chest with his fist, that sent her skidding backwards right across the ward. But I swear she was scrabbling to get back to him while she was still sliding

(*Top*) The author on leave in November 1918 and (*bottom*) in plain clothes with his mother.

backwards on her bottom across the ward floor. As soon as she had stopped sliding she got up and went right back at him, shouting for orderlies, but not waiting for them to appear. The man on the other side of the delirious man and I, on my side, both started to get out of our beds to help, but we were neither of us of any use because, as soon as our feet touched the floor, we both collapsed like wet sacks. However, two orderlies came running within seconds and managed to restrain the patient. Then we were picked up and put back in our beds and given something to put us to sleep. When we woke up again the next morning, the bed between us was empty. I suppose the attack of delirium was the final flare-up before the chap died. But I shall never forget that girl getting up and going right back at her patient, who was twice her size and weight.

I heard other stories of nurses' devotion too, from friends who were in a tent hospital at Camiers, when it was bombed from the air; stories of girls flinging themselves on their patients and trying to protect them with their own bodies in default of any other protection. My admiration for hospital nurses is deep and sincere, but not, I think, unreasoning. They did a marvellous job in the war and still do in peace. If you are lucky, you do not need a nurse's services very often, but when you do, you need them damned badly and I think we should express our admiration more frequently and more tangibly than we do. We might at least give them reasonable salaries, though the gifts they give their patients are not the sort that can be bought for money.

The fellow who was suffering from concussion gave us a lot of interest and amusement, because he was so lucid and logical even in his wildest ramblings. He complained bitterly at first at being put in a ward full of Indian other ranks rather than in a British officers' ward. Later, he became much happier and told us, in great detail, how four stretcher-bearers had taken him out of that ward and carried him upstairs into this new ward on the first floor with its nice verandah, which he liked very much. As it was only a tent hospital with no upstairs and no verandah of any sort, we could not imagine what had put these ideas into his head. In actual fact, he had never been moved out of the bed he had been put into when he arrived.

I cannot remember how long I was in hospital, but when I got out, I found that the battalion had moved up to Enghien, about twenty kilometres south-west of Brussels. The men were billeted in a large school, which they did not like. They much preferred to be billeted in farms and cottages where they could get on terms with the inhabitants and have some sort of semblance of a home life. They had more room in the school and were warm and dry, but it was just like a barracks and our men were by this time practically all civilians in uniform with almost no regulars left among them.

We settled down to a peace-time routine which was extraordinarily dull. The Army is a fighting machine and, when it is not fighting or training to fight, it is difficult to find things to do to keep the men from getting bored. We organised games and concerts and so on, but it was up-hill work and not very successful. Everyone was tired to death of the war and the Army and the only thing that really mattered was when one could get home.

One example of this war-weariness and lethargy was an expedition that we tried to organise to visit the battlefield of Waterloo. We thought this might arouse some interest, but the men said they had seen all the battlefields they ever wanted to see and were not going to traipse off to see another one, however historically important.

We were instructed to lecture the men one half-hour every day on 'Current Affairs'. It seemed to me too ridiculous that I, who had gone into the Army straight from school and knew nothing whatever of life or politics, should lecture men old enough to be my father on the political and economic situation. I didn't know anything about it, anyway. What I did with my little lot was to tell them to sit down and smoke, while I read them the third leader from *The Times*, which was usually mildly humorous, for five minutes. Then we just sat and talked till the half-hour was up. I don't think it did much good, but also, I don't think it did as much harm as if I had tried to imbue them with any particular political doctrine.

The only incidents of any importance were a thoroughly justified mutiny and a big ceremonial parade in Brussels before the King of the Belgians.

The mutiny started at breakfast time with a sudden order that all officers were to go down to their companies at once, as the men had refused to parade for a route-march. We went down to the school, wondering what it was all about but not really apprehensive that we should be massacred en masse by rioting troops. It turned out that the men were perfectly amiably disposed towards their officers and had no intention of rioting but were just fed up – in my opinion, quite justifiably.

The root cause of the trouble was the delay in demobilisation. On top of that, we had recently been reduced to eating iron rations – bully beef and biscuits – because of a strike of the engine drivers on the railway; people who had been drawing six bob a day all through the war as against the infantryman's one shilling and who had never seen a shot fired or even got their feet wet. Our men were justly incensed that they should have had to go on to iron rations because of a strike by these people who had never really seen the war. The route-march was only a minor grievance, but the last straw that broke the camel's back. Our men felt that they had marched all over France on their own flat feet for years and years because they had to, but they did not see any need to go on doing it now that the war was over.

It was all settled quite amicably. The route-march was diplomatically cut down to a mere five miles or so and it was explained that a certain amount of exercise was necessary to keep everyone fit in case the Boche turned nasty and broke the Armistice. Better food was provided as soon as possible and lectures were given on the demobilisation procedure. It wasn't a real mutiny in the generally accepted sense, but just a little explosion of discontent about quite legitimate grievances.

The ceremonial parade in Brussels was in the nature of a formal welcome back of the King of the Belgians to his capital. King Albert had never left Belgian soil or pandered to the Boche and was popular both with his own people and their allies. The parade was held on a bitterly cold day in January and the horses were slipping and sliding about all over the frosty cobbles. I was glad when it was decided that only two officers per battalion should be mounted, so that I did not have to try and control a horse under these conditions. I had been doing a good deal of riding at

Enghien, but was by no means an expert horseman.

We marched through streets lined with the cheering populace and the King took the salute in front of the Royal Palace. One interesting difference between the attitudes of the two armies came to light. We had scrubbed our equipment until it was almost white and polished the brass till it shone. The Belgians even thought that we had been issued with new equipment for the occasion, but it was not so – it was just the old Army spit and polish.

The Belgians, on the other hand, posed as veteran warriors and pretended that they had come straight on to parade from the battlefield. Neither the King nor his staff had shaved. They looked thoroughly scruffy and disreptuable and this must have been done deliberately, because Belgian officers normally look as smart as those of any other nation.

One thing displeased me personally. I heard a woman in the crowd say to her companion as I passed '*Regardes le petit capitaine, là. Qu'il est jeune.*' As I regarded myself as a real old soldier and had service chevrons half way up my sleeve, I was pretty disgusted with her lack of perspicacity.

One good thing this parade did for me though was to make me a lot of friends. Instead of being billeted in schools and large halls, the troops were, as a matter of policy, billeted in ones and twos on private houses. I had the job of arranging the billets and people would stop me in the streets when they saw what I was doing and say 'Can you let me have a soldier to stay in my house?' The result was that I got to know a number of people and after the parade there were at least half-a-dozen houses at which I could turn up, without warning, and ask for a bed for the night. That was most useful, because whenever I could get a few hours' leave, I could lorry-hop into Brussels and be sure of a welcome.

The Belgians, generally, were glad to see us and were very good to us. An exception was my landlady at Enghien, who did not appear to have a very high opinion of the British officer as a species. I remember coming in once after I had been playing football and had been knocked over into a cow pat. I admit I did not smell very sweetly, but from the way she looked at me one might have thought I had been rolling in the muck for pleasure.

On another occasion, I had been riding in the park at Enghien. We were galloping down a sloping meadow and at the bottom was a patch of flood water lying in a hollow. I tried to pull my horse up, but he was excited by the other horses galloping behind and would take no notice. As I could not stop him, I thought we would have to jump it, but at the last moment he dug his fore-legs in and stopped more quickly than I should have thought possible. I didn't; I just sailed over his head and landed on my back in the middle of the water splash. I was not hurt, but my landlady did not approve of my bedraggled state when I crawled home.

We did not have a bad time at Enghien, but the question of demobilisation overshadowed everything and was the only thing that people were interested in. The men felt, quite naturally, that as the PBI had had the worst time during the war, they should be sent home first. And, among them, that the order of release should be determined primarily by length of service. On the other hand, the Powers-that-be wanted home first the men who had special skills and could get industry going again. These two opposed points of view were more or less reconciled by a system of points being allotted, some for length of service and some for civilian skills and the order of release was based on these point tables. The whole thing was laid down on paper but the details were not made generally available.

In February 1919, I was made Demobilisation Officer for the battalion, which meant that I had access to these tables of priorities and had to work out the order of release for the various categories. I found that students had a high priority. I was not exactly a student, but I had only just left school when the war began and had no other trade or profession, so I decided to call myself a student. With the high priority accorded to students plus the unusually large number of points due to me for long service, I found myself at the top of the list and almost the first person I demobilised was myself.

This was highly satisfactory, but the Army took one last kick at us on the final journey home. The railways were running by this time and when we went down to the station we were delighted to find a real home-side GWR train waiting for us. It had glass in all the windows and real cushions on the seats. We had not travelled in such luxury for years. Unfortunately, someone had forgotten, or been unable, to connect up the heating apparatus with the engine. There was snow on the ground and we got colder and colder. At one of the many unscheduled stops, we raided a stack in a farm-yard and got straw to put on the floor, but even this did not help much. Then we got to a place where a hot meal was supposed to be laid on for us, but the meat was so bad that it stank to high heaven and could not possibly be eaten. Somebody ought to have been shot for that, but we were so nearly out of the Army that we did not even bother to teach the idle cooks a lesson. One of the men in my compartment had a tin of sardines in his haversack and we shared this between the six of us, taking it in turns to lift out one sardine by its tail and eat it as though it were a stalk of asparagus. And that is all we had till we got into a camp at Dunkerque late that night.

The next day we were de-loused, which involved taking a hot shower in one hut and then running naked across the snow-covered ground to another, where we were issued with clean under-clothes. But these were all minor trials and tribulations compared with the one outstanding fact that we were on our way home and were definitely going to get shot of the Army for ever and ever, Amen. We could endure anything the Army could do to us in those last hours, braced, as we were, by the knowledge that, within a day or so, we should be able to thumb our noses at the whole damned organisation.

The demobilisation procedure was short, as well as sweet, and within a couple of days of landing in England, we were free men.

That was the end of my war. I did not regret my early demobilisation and I was definitely glad that I did not accept the permanent commission that I was offered. Some of my friends did, but they were almost all thrown out of the Army a year or two later because of the vicious cuts wielded by the 'Geddes axe'.* All they gained was that they had to start their civilian careers some years later than their contemporaries. This was hard luck because, when they accepted 'permanent' commissions, they thought

* The measures introduced by the committee on national expenditure in 1922, presided over by Sir Eric Geddes, drastically reducing the armed forces.

that 'permanent' meant what it said. They did not allow for the politicians' habit of altering the meanings of words to suit themselves.

In these notes, I have tried to reflect the thoughts and feelings we had at the time and not to allow myself to be affected too much by hindsight and second thoughts. But there seems to me to have been one particular difference between the First and Second World Wars in the matter of propaganda and its results. There was a lot of rot put out by politicians and newspapers in both wars, of course, but I do not think we were so much affected by it in the First War.

It may be that it was more skilfully used in the Second War. Or it may be that, as a civilian, I was more exposed to it.

In the First War, it is true that, having no wireless or television and seldom seeing a newspaper, the troops, and I can speak only for the men in the line, were insulated from a great deal of the hot air that was circulated. But even when propaganda was directed definitely at the men, it did not seem to have much effect.

There was, for instance, a certain Colonel who used to go round giving most bloodthirsty lectures on bayonet-fighting and allied subjects. He was supposed to rouse the fighting spirit in the troops and make them long to be 'up and at 'em'. The men listened to him because they had to, but I think most of them thought he was quite unnecessarily bloody-minded. They knew enough of the beastliness of war from actual experience, without having theoretical horrors rammed down their throats when they were out of the line and they just didn't want to hear about the best methods of twisting a bayonet in a man's guts so as to do the greatest possible amount of damage.

And it certainly made no difference in their attitude towards the Boche. It was agreed that the Germans were pests who had upset all our lives and who had to be put down so that they could never do it again. But there was very little hatred of the individual German soldier. In fact, once he was captured and therefore made harmless, he became almost a pet, instead of a pest. He was called 'Poor old Jerry' and offered cigarettes and tea and no one even contemplated twisting a bayonet in his guts.

The Boche soldier, on the other hand, seemed to be more af-

B.A.R. Shore and the author, 1919.

fected by propaganda that his enemies were ravening and callous beasts, devoid of all humanity. Prisoners were often very frightened when they were first captured. I remember that at one time I was examining German prisoners' papers. I could not read German – all I was doing was taking their papers off them and sending them down in charge of the escorts so that the prisoners could not destroy any information they might have on them before it could reach the hands of our Intelligence people.

Incidentally, almost every one of the prisoners that I examined was carrying one or more pornographic postcards. I had quite an education looking at them, but they all had to go down to Intelligence because many of them had addresses on them, which would reveal people in French towns who had been aiding the enemy.

But this is by the way. What I was going to say was that I was sitting at a table and, because my revolver was pressing uncomfortably into my stomach, I took it out of the holster and laid it on the table in front of me. Immediately, the prisoner under examination threw his hands in the air and babbled '*Kamerade, kamerade*'. He was quite pale with fright and obviously thought that I was going to shoot him then and there in cold blood.

I should not have expected to be shot like that if I had been captured by the Boche. I might have been killed in being captured, but once I had surrendered and been marched away for interrogation, I should not have expected to have been shot out of hand. Why did the Boche? Was he more susceptible to propaganda or had he been more exposed to it? I don't know, but it does seem to me that our people tended to keep their feet on the ground and form their own opinions more than most.

I do not regret having had to go through the war. I was lucky in that it came to me at a time of life when I was physically at my best and still had the resilience of youth to help overcome the more unpleasant aspects of it. It carried me over the transition from boyhood to manhood; a difficult period that would, I suppose, have normally been bridged by a few years at a university. I regard the war as part of my education – but a more intensive course in living than could have been provided by any university.

I was never a good soldier. In the whole of my military career, I only received two compliments, but, since one of them was due to no merit of mine and does bring back certain memories, I think it can be mentioned here. I was told that a group of the men were overheard discussing the shortcomings of their officers and one of them, referring to me, said: 'No, that little one don't know much, but he's always about when it comes on to shell.'

Normally, I should have been very proud to have had that said of me. But no one knew better than I did that, if I did turn up when 'it came on to shell', it was because I had been ordered to the scene and not in the least because I wanted to be there. In actual fact, these incidents provided some of the most unpleasant moments of the whole war.

In theory, there should have always been at least one officer on duty in the front line. But numbers were so short that often this was not physically possible. Much of the time we were down to the Company Commander and two subalterns in C Company and, on occasions, to only one. When this happened, the front line just had to be left when things were quiet, because even subalterns have to eat and sleep sometimes. That was when the worst moments occurred.

You would be back in the Company HQ dug-out, perhaps getting some hot soup or cocoa inside you after hours out in the cold and the wet or perhaps even stretched out on a bunk for a much-needed spot of sleep, when, suddenly, all Hell would break loose above ground. You would shut your ears and eyes and concentrate on ignoring the racket, hoping against hope and all experience that, by doing so, you could make it go away. But it never did and within seconds you would hear the fateful words from the Company Commander that you had been dreading, though you knew they were bound to come. 'Nettleton, would you like to go up and see what all that noise is about?'

It was a most horrible moment. Your heart sank into the pit of your stomach, while your mind thought, 'Why doesn't he send someone else? Or go himself for a change? Why does it have to be me?' But you had to repress these thoughts while you struggled into your equipment and shouted for your runner, though your mind went on conjuring up the most horrible visions. You did not know what to expect, so, naturally, expected the worst. It might be nothing more than a pointless 'hate', with everybody very frightened but no real damage done, but your imagination painted scenes of carnage, with ghastly casualties to be dealt with and whole lengths of blown-in trench to be repaired and reorganised. Or it might be a raid, with the trench full of Boche bombers. It might be anything or nothing. All you knew was that you did not want to go and find out.

By the time your runner appeared, you would have taken your tin hat off its nail, picked up a Verey pistol from the table and started to climb the greasy steps, trying not to tread on more than you could help of the sleeping bodies with which they were littered.

Once outside, the worst was over. You had to pause for a minute to listen and try to assess where the centre of the disturbance was and the best way to get there. The mere fact of doing something or, at least having to think what to do, blunted the sharp edge of fear.

But nothing ever blunted the edge of those moments when you were waiting for the order that you knew must come.

The only slightly satisfactory feature of the whole situation was that, when you did appear in the front line, you were always made very welcome. Not only when there were alarums and excursions, but even when things were quiet, it seemed that your just being there did help, even if you did no more than climb on the fire-step beside a sentry and peer with him into the darkness.

Being on sentry duty at night was a nervy business and that is why we always had two men on together, if possible, or at least a second man on the fire-step, within reach of the sentry's boot. One's own wire always seemed much too thin to be effective and the broken and cratered ground made it hard to detect if there was anyone out there or not. A lump of earth might be just a lump of earth or a Boche's head or bottom. And a rat running over it might be just that or a Boche preparing to throw a bomb at you. The old joke that, after half an hour, you could see the wire posts forming fours was almost literally true. And if one nervous sentry fired a shot, it would set off a ripple of fire both ways up and down the line, though no one knew what he was firing at. It was one of the jobs of the officer on duty to stop this waste of ammunition when there was no reason for it.

The rats were a menace. They seemed almost as big as rabbits with all the food they got from unburied corpses and they were as bold as brass. At Bully-Grenay, when we were with the Royal Naval Division, a rat ate right through B.A.R. Shore's haversack while he slept with his equipment on him. And an Army webbing haversack takes a bit of nibbling through. One tried to bury corpses near the parapet, but one could only chuck the body into a shell-hole and shovel some earth on top of it. I remember burying one chap twice in one night like this and each time he was thrown out of his makeshift grave within a short time by shell-fire. The third time this happened, I gave up and let him lie unburied.

Wiring was another hazardous and frightening task. When I first went into the line with the RND, we were still using wooden posts that had to be hammered into the ground with a mallet. Though one put a folded sand-bag on top of the post to deaden the sound, one seemed to make enough noise to wake the dead. The screw-pickets that came into use later on were a great improvement, in that they could be screwed into the earth by means of a merkin-handle passed through a loop at the top. But, even so, a wiring party always seemed to make an unconscionable amount of noise. Barbed wire is difficult stuff to handle even in a level field in daylight. In the dark, on cratered ground and with the whole party in a state of jitters, it was impossible to do it silently. The stuff wrapped itself round your legs and ripped your clothes and your flesh and the oaths of the people whose hands were getting torn to pieces were added to by the curses of the NCOs telling them to be quiet.

I think I preferred being in the covering party, lying right out in front, to being in the wiring party itself. At least, you were lying down and stood a good chance of seeing the enemy before they could see you. And though the covering party could normally prevent any Jerries getting close enough to throw bombs at the wiring party, they could do nothing to stop enemy machine-guns opening up with devastating effect. You cannot dodge bullets with barbed wire festooned all round you and the more you plunge about seeking cover, the more you get entangled with, and ripped to pieces by, the beastly stuff. The covering party only had to lie flat and make sure that no raiding party was allowed to get to close quarters and mop up the disorganised mob of the wiring party. And all that several nights of this nerve-racking work served to produce never seemed to be more than a sparse and rickety fence that an old lady in a crinoline could have walked through.

The REs, working in back areas in daylight could build magnificent entanglements, but the wiring in front of the front line, where it was most needed, never seemed anything like adequate, however much work was put into it.

These notes have been written in dribs and drabs over a period of about four months, but, on reading them over, it seems to me that a definite pattern emerges. When I was in the Artists, I was a school-boy and I enjoyed the 'gang spirit' as any boy does. A young male likes to be part of a gang. It helps him when he is still too young to be able to face the world on his own and he draws strength and self-confidence from the gang.

When I went up to join the RB, I was deprived of this support and, standing on my own feet for the first time, I found them an excessively weak and wobbly platform. But the muscles grew stronger, as muscles do, by being exercised. I did not like accepting responsibility any more than the next man, but I found myself in situations where I had to exercise it, simply because there was no one else I could push it on to and these situations cropped up more frequently than they would have done in civil life. Moreover, they were more clear-cut and the consequences of failure were more immediately obvious. You coped with the situation in front of you because you had to. There was no one else to do so and if you didn't cope, the consequences were staring you in the face and there was no safety in hiding your head in the sand and refusing to face them. Therefore you learnt and learnt fast. If you did not, you were soon in a position where you could not learn any more in this world.

I think that two of the most important lessons I learned were:

1. That the other fellow is at least as much afraid of you, and

The author five years after the war.

possibly more so, than you are of him.

2. In a sticky situation, it is better to give an order, almost any order, than just to do nothing. You cannot always control circumstances, but it is always best to have a shot at it. You may or may not succeed. You may be overwhelmed, whatever you do; but if you do nothing, you are damned well sure to be.

These lessons apply to civil as well as military life. But in war they are impressed on you more frequently and more forcibly than in civil life. You learn in a few months what in civil life might take years, because the lessons are in plain black and white and are presented without any disguise or pretty wrapping. And I think the four years I spent learning them were not wasted.

I never cease to give thanks for my luck in coming through the war unscathed and not having to learn far harder lessons through living a life of permanent invalidism with a mutilated body or mind.

APPENDIX

Appendix

Diary of my First Trip to the Line.
Originally written in pencil in my Field Service Notebook.
Small parties of men of the Artists Rifles who were going in for commissions were sent up the line to have a look at the war before they were gazetted. Our party was attached to the Anson Battalion of the Naval Division at Bully-Grenay, just south of Lens. B.A.R. Shore was the only other member of the Signal Section in our party. Bully-Grenay was a very quiet sector. That's why it was chosen for introducing people to the line.

30/8/16. Wed. Left by motor-bus (from Hesdin) at 11.00 am. Arrived Bully about 3.15 pm. Reserve trenches same night. Raining hard, water above ankles in some places. Attached, with Elston, to A coy. No 4 Platoon. (Mr Jones & Sgt. Pickering). Most uncomfortable night, but no duties.

31/8/16. Thurs. Fine. RE fatigue in morning, deepening and levelling communication trenches. Rifle and gas inspection at 9am. Fatigue 10am to 12:15pm. and 3:15 to 6pm. Got shelled when we began, so had to retire and wait for a bit.

1/9/16 Fine. Guard 3am to 6am.
6 to 9am. Breakfast, clean rifle and trench.
9 to 12 noon. R.E. Carrying fatigue. Visit from Capt. Bare. German anti-aircraft gunnery good.
Afternoon. Slept.
9pm to 1:30am. Handing sandbags out of a sap in front line. Back breaking work and trenches very muddy. (Memo — When leading working parties or bodies of men about trenches, move slowly, especially at night, or party will be split up.)

2nd. Sat: 9am. Rifle and gas helmet inspection.
9:15 to 11:30. RE carrying fatigue. Twice up to Mechanics and back, carrying timber and sandbags. Parapet of communication trench blown in just before we came along it. Probably 3" high-explosive shells.
Very tired this morning and got snotted for nearly going to sleep during Stand-to. Iron helmets very heavy when one is tired.
[*What actually happened, though I didn't put it in my diary at the time, was that I was standing on the fire-step with my head drooping on the parapet, sound asleep, when an officer came by on his rounds and gave me a welt across the bottom with his cane. Quite irregular, but far more effective than if he had put me on a charge, as is proved by the fact that I still remember the incident and that I felt no resentment at the time.*]
Afternoon. Slept.
5 to 9pm. Carried gas cylinders from Support Dump in Morrow trench to Col's House on Arras Road. Heaviest work we have done yet.

Sunday 3rd: Guard 3 to 5am. Relieved by 4th Bedfords about 8am. Their Coy filed in and we filed out about five minutes later. Bath after lunch and inspection by MO for scabies. Beastly billet right up in attic; only ventilation two small holes where tiles have been knocked off. Dirty and smelly. BAR and Moore in same building in room below. Only washing accommodation is a bucket if you can borrow or steal one. Nothing doing. In evening went out to SW of town and had a talk with an R.G.A. man, who shewed the gun positions. Looked at a French gun.

Monday 4th:
Slept till nearly seven. BAR saw Capt Bare. Apparently we have got to live with our platoons and do ordinary work until the next time in the trenches, when we will interview our Coy Commanders. Hope to be in same Coy as BAR as Moore is willing to change. Excellent stew for lunch. Lay on grass outside town all afternoon and wrote diary and letters. Evening, dined out – on eggs and chips.

Tuesday, 5th: Heard BAR was carrying barbed wire last night till two this morning. Still raining. Spoke to Sgt Viner and his crew who have had an exciting time. We shall go into firing line on Thursday and in our next four days rest probably get attached to Sigs as Bare has spoken about it.

Wednesday, 6th: Fatigue to trenches finished about 1am. Got some soup at Brigade Soup Kitchen. Good idea! Another fatigue in afternoon 1:30 to 7pm. Finished early and cut away because I had a lot to do. Left washing and some spare clothes at a beastly little hole at the back of the billet. D Coy went to spend the night at Mechanics. Bought butter, potted meat and sardines for trenches. Singing in billet till late.

Thursday 7th: Breakfast 4:30am. Fall in at 5. Come down right round by Arras Road and Col's House. Went into Kellet Trench. Spoke to Mr Jones about a swop. About 9:30 am, Moore came along with a chit. Join BAR in D Coy. Topping little dug-out to ourselves. On a periscope from 10 to 11 am. 11:30 am hit on back by dirt thrown up by a shell. First event.
1 hour on and 3 off during day; 2 hours on and 2 off during night, when there are two on together. From 11 to 12 midnight, BAR went on a wiring party. Saw Sgt: Viner in the evening.

Friday 8th: Watch 3 to 5 am. Stand-to 5 to 6. then two hours on periscope and six off throughout day.
8 to 10 am. On watch.
10 am to 1 pm. Slept.
11.45 to 11.48 am. 3 mins bombardment by our artillery. Did not hear a sound. Seems to be a difficulty in getting water up. From 6 to 8 am we sent over toffee-apples and they replied with rifle grenades. Damaged the trenches near the trench-mortar battery a bit but no casualties.
While on watch this morning a stoat came right down beside me.
Last night, about 10 pm we shelled a German armoured train, which replied feebly.

Saturday, 9th. Thirst in the land. No water for tea or drinking till

the afternoon. Been extremely thirsty since yesterday breakfast time. Ration of water is 2 pints per diem – not enough for me and when these do not turn up I get fed up with life. However, double ration turned up in the afternoon.
11 to 12 midday. Digging and cleaning trench fatigue. Afternoon slept. 4 to 6 pm on periscope.
8 to 9 pm. Stand-to.
9 to 11 pm. on watch.
11 to 12 midnight. Sleep.
12 to 3.30 am. On listening post on No: 16 Sap, armed with two Mills bombs and trench stick. No steel helmets. Quite exciting for first half hour but nearly went to sleep before it was over. Kept awake by one of our own machine-guns which played so close to us that it kept sending earth all over us. Got in one hour's sleep before stand-to at 5 am. Very tired but interesting experience.

Sunday, 10th: Sergt took a bomb to bits to shew me and then threw it away. Took another to bits to shew BAR, couldn't get detonator back and had to throw that away as well.
Detonator of Mills bomb contains 1/16th oz of Fulminate of Mercury. The red paint marks on the bomb shew where the layer of Ammonal is in the bomb.
Fairly smashed up trench just below us with Rifle Grenades.
Several splinters came near us but chiefly blow-backs from our own toffee-apples.
Stunt on this evening to capture a prisoner.
10 pm. Artillery begin a terrific bombardment while two officers and some bombers wait in Sap 18. Artillery gave what is called a box-barrage, beginning at a pre-arranged time and continuing as long as we sent up red lights. Ammunition fired in the ten minutes or quarter of an hour for which the raid lasted, comprised approximately:

Light Field Artillery	1200 rounds
Heavy (60 lbs)	100 rounds
2-inch Trench Mortars	700 rounds

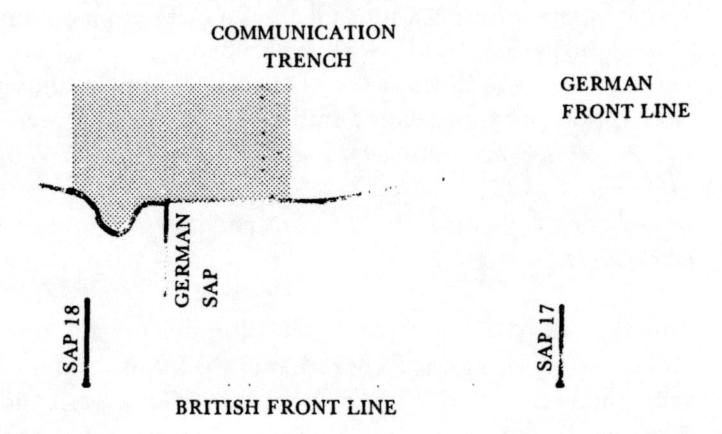

Artillery gave box-barrage on shaded portion to isolate the German sap from any assistance. Some few Germans rushed up the sap to escape our shells; when our men came, they had either to stay in the sap and be killed or captured or else run back to either right or left along the firing line (probably to right as there is no communication trench for some distance on left) and be blown to bits in the inferno of bursting shells which was all over shaded area.

Artillery did not begin at a prearranged time. Bombing party (2 officers and 12 men) went out together. One half stayed at German sap head; others went down to cut off retreat. When both parties were ready, they sent up a red light and artillery began. Men in our trenches kept sending up red lights until all our men were safely back.

Bombing party go out along sunken road; one half to German sap-head, the other to cut off retreat of Germans down sap. Six or seven Germans in sap, all get away except one, a sniper, wounded, who is brought back. Our casualties; – 1 officer and 1 Leading Seaman, slightly wounded. Prisoner turns out to be a Saxon of 127 Reserve. The artillery had to keep on as long as our red lights were going up. Two green lights were sent up to tell furthest advanced party to close in and cut off retreat.

Bombardment was terrible – levelled their wire so that you could walk over it like a road. First thoughts were how absolutely bloody

it was, then wind up a bit and then a calm appreciation of it all. Enemy answered feebly with whizz-bangs and rifle grenades, but chiefly on our reserves. Very glad to have seen it all, but it defies description and transcends anything I had ever imagined.
(*If the above account seems a trifle confused, it is because of differences between what was intended and what actually happened, which I learnt about in bits and pieces from various people afterwards.*)

Monday, 11th: Ration party till 12 midnight and so only about two hours sleep again. Relieved about 6.30 or 7 am by Howe battalion and retire to dug-out at Mechanics. Get a wash and clean my foot, which has been sore. At one this morning I could not put it to the ground, but now it is clean it is already better. Lie about with BAR all morning; very sleepy.
Bombardment early this morning, beginning about two am, towards Loos.
12 noon. Watch has been going for over two hours.
Afternoon. Went to Bully to get supplies and washing. Got round the Chief to let us go. Arranged with BAR's friend (O.C. Dugouts) to take us round with him on Wednesday morning. Letter from Bruin; seems doubtful if we shall get back into the Section rooms.

Tuesday, 12th: Received parcel from Uncle Ernest. Nothing doing. Foot still very painful.
Afternoon. One journey to LTM battery with ammunition. Hung the box on my rifle and nearly broke my shoulder.
Expect gun has a bit of a curve in it. Talked to Capt Douglas in evening. Tried to spot our gun positions while they were firing but could not see a sign of one, despite the fact that I could see every inch of ground for more than a square mile and that I knew the guns were there.
Brought stopping out of left lower jaw tooth. It will probably give me gyp in a day or two.

Wednesday, 13th: Went round dugouts with Mr – of 1st Marines. Saw beginning of trench mortar emplacement. Air in one shaft was so bad that they had to pump air down into it. Wrote up notes and letters in afternoon, BAR carried Stokes Gun ammunition down.

Thursday, 14th: Nothing till one when we went up to Bully. Bought bread, butter and chocolate and got the photos, which were rotten as I expected. Had a very nice tea with Mr Prynne. Everyone has to take packs into trenches in future – points to an attack or may be merely winter routine.

Friday, 15th: Parade in a panic at 5.50 am. Move a hundred yards or so down Mechanics and wait till 6.40 am. BAR goes to B Coy, I go to C. Sleep all day, chill on stomach, sick as a dog just before I go on watch, but that seems to put things right. Am attached to Mr Webly (12 Platoon) as runner. He seems to have only just arrived in trenches. All officers turn out at stand-to and then take watches of two hours on and as many as possible off. If you go over the top, you get the rest of the night in.

Saturday 16th: Stand-to at quarter to five. Finish at about seven until twelve. Murray and Mr Blackmoor went out to investigate a covered in crater found the night before.

Sunday, 17th: Slept all through stand-to and went on watch at ten. Found men in 17 Sap had tried to cut into walls of sap and broken into an old French mine. Entrance originally from firing trench; blocked for about seven yards and then free for about seven yards. Top of mine level with bottom of sap; mine about three feet deep. Going out to-night to reconnoitre ground between 17–18 sap.
Evening. Left 18 Sap about 9.45 pm and crawled about on our bellies till we nearly ran into our own wire. Struck out again and examined mine crater and old tree opposite Mr Webly's dugout. Came in, by mistake, below 17 Sap. The Major and others were firing up lights from the sap and thinking we had got lost, which was pretty nearly true. Our wire seemed to be all chevaux-de-frise and little plantations, not more than a foot or so high.

Monday, 18th: Relieved and marched straight through tons of mud to Hersin-Coupigny without a halt. Billeted very close in huts, two layers deep. Went and had grub in a decent little estaminet afternoon and evening. Mud everywhere. First decent people for three weeks and they are not much to boast about.

Tuesday, 19th: Parade in the morning and saw a bus go by, but it was not for us. Marched about 15 miles with all our goods & chattels via Fresencourt, Rebreuve, La Comté, Bajus to Diéval. (15 Miles). At Rebreuve, we were inspected by the Corps Commander. Lunch on a hilltop just before La Comté. Raining all the time and v. cold. Glad to get in. Blanket and rum ration and straw to sleep on. Absolute luxury, best sleep since I left Hesdin.

Wednesday 20th: Did not get up till seven. Only washing water was that from cess-pit in farmyard. Waited all day for the bus. 'Hope deferred maketh the heart sick.' It does, very.

Thursday 21st: I think we shall all walk home if the bus does not come soon. Live on omelettes, coffee and bouchets.

Friday, 22nd: Walked to St Pol (6 miles). Had all our kit carried for us on limber and Bare's valise. Passed château at Bryas. Tea at St Pol and time to look round. Decent town. Came home by leave train. Jolly glad to have got here at last.

Postscript

Whilst preparing for a second edition of my father's book, *The Anger of the Guns*, I visited the archives of The Royal Greenjackets (the regiment into which The Rifle Brigade has now been incorporated). The knowledgeable archivist, Major R. D. Cassidy MBE, kindly guided me through the records for the relevant period. These consisted of the general history of The Rifle Brigade, which had many battalions, and the more specific daily reports from my father's battalion – 2nd RB.

These daily reports were hand written in the trenches each day by the adjutant or CO but unsigned. They were on rough, stained message paper. As I turned the pages I was suddenly astounded to recognise my father's handwriting. I could vividly imagine my twenty year old father, crouched in his dugout, with the rattle of small arms fire and the crump of shells above, writing by the light of a guttering candle. It was a moving moment.

My father actually wrote the reports himself for the periods August 31 to September 18 1917, October 1 to November 6 1917, and January 15 to January 30 1918. (After this date the reports are no longer handwritten but have been subsequently typed.) These must have been the times when he was acting as adjutant. A copy of a page is shown on p. 210.

Set out below are some extracts from these reports which amplify and confirm my father's recollections. (The actual wording of the reports is in italics, with page references to the book itself. My comments are in brackets.)

Nov. 23 1916 — *2/Lt Nettleton reported for duty.*

March 4 1917 (see p. 64-5) — *The POW party consisted of 2/Lt Nettleton and 20 ORs* (other ranks). *Casualties were 1 man killed and 3 wounded* (presumably the men stationed at the crossroads). *Only 40*

POWs were collected.

August 12 1917 (see p. 95)
During the day Lt. Nettleton made a reconnaissance of the country with guides to lead up the Royal Irish Rifles and Royal Berks to the position of the attack.

August 17 1917 (see p. 99)
Capt. Curtis being slightly wounded since 14th and very exhausted was left behind at old Bn HQ with Lt. Nettleton to help.

Jan. 6 1918
2/Lt Nettleton's mention in dispatches published in the London Gazette.

May 25 1918 (see p. 136 et seq)
German attack started...... 60 details went up at 12 am (sic) *under 2/Lt Ellis who was killed. 44 ORs went up under Capt Boughton-Leigh and 2/Lt Nettleton at 8pm.*

May 27 1918
.....remains of 25th Brigade staff having practically ceased to exist. In the evening the 8th Div collected a scratch force from all sources available and placed the resultant 500 men under 75th Brigade Capt Boughton-Leigh – 2/Lt Nettleton and 44 ORs moving up to form part of the force..

May 30 1918 (see p. 146)
The battalion report here confirms that the casualties for May 27 to 30 were 27 officers and 680 ORs

July 25 1918
Left hand salute abolished. (!)

Feb 3 1919 (see p. 186)
General training. Lts Nettleton and Robinson demobilized.

Postscript

My father was in the army for just over four years, mostly in the trenches, reported missing in May 1918, and wounded three times. He was obviously a competent and courageous officer, being charged with several independent tasks, often acting as adjutant, and receiving a "mention in dispatches". Finally he was offered a regular commision, which he declined.

J. O. Nettleton
July 2003

Oct 21st Battn relieved 2nd Lincolnshire Regt in front line WARNETON Sector. C & D Coys in front line, B in support C in Reserve. Battn H.Q. St YVES.

Oct 22nd Intermittent shelling. Work. A & part of B Coy carried. Remainder of B Coy assisted front line Coys with work. Casualties 1 OR wounded by shell fire

Oct 23rd Continued shelling & TM fire on BASSE VILLE + front line. Casualties 2 OR killed 12 wounded. Work as for 22nd
2/LT A.G. Tyndall
2/LT J Brooker } Joined for duty.
2/LT G.E. Collins

Oct 24th Intermittent shelling & TM fire. Casualties 3 OR wounded. 2/LT D.F.W. Baden-Powell joined for duty.

Oct 25th Less shelling than two previous days. Casualties 1 OR wounded.

Oct 26th Quiet day. 2/LT J.E. Lund slightly wounded on patrol.

Oct 27th Quiet day. No casualties.

Oct 28th Quiet day except for TM fire at 9 pm 2/LT [illegible] & party of 25 OR raided enemy trenches under artillery barrage. They succeeded in entering enemy trenches & killing one German, but the remainder of garrison of the post raided ran away while our party was getting through the wire. [illegible] casualties in the raid were:-
1 OR missing believed blown up by shell
5 OR slightly wounded.
Other casualties during day:-
3 OR. killed by TM fire on a front line post

Oct 29th After dawn very quiet day indeed. 3 OR wounded by shell fire. Battn was relieved by 1st Bn Worcester Regt & moved into DE SEULE Camp.
2/LT. H Coles
2/LT C H Sidney } Joined for duty.
2/LT A R A Woodward

Daily Battalion Reports 1917 - written by the author